ABOUT HER

LEARNING TO LOVE BY FINDING AND DEFINING SELF-LOVE

MAURICE L. BROWN

EDITED BY EVA RYAN

ISBN (Print): 979-8-9912332-0-0

ISBN (eBook): 979-8-9912332-1-7

Cover Art Design: Fariss Ryan

Illustrations: Images created with the assistance of DALL·E 2

TABLE OF CONTENTS

First and foremost, I would like to dedicate this book to my daughter.

There's a line in one of my poems which reads, "Funny how raising you has flipped the script and simultaneously indulged in raising me."

Not only did your immediate existence forever change the trajectory of my life in the obvious ways, but your presence consistently inspires me to reflect on my relationships with women. It is through this reflection I have been able to grow as a man. Hopefully, this piece of art will paint a picture for you. I hope it helps you make sense of the abstract from my frame of mind. Hang it in view of your mind's eye to gain perspective as you cultivate your own relationships.

Secondly, I dedicate this book to my mothers and sisters. Through their experiences I have been able to develop a moral compass. They continue to guide me and serve as a point of reference as I navigate through life.

Lastly, I dedicate this book to every woman who has been a part of my journey. Whether it be physically, spiritually, emotionally, or any combination of the three. I have come to realize the contributions each of you have played, both consciously and unconsciously, in the man who I am today.

PROLOGUE

Like most dictionaries depict it, I only knew love as a deep feeling of affection.

Wait...

LLLLLLLLLLLLLLLLLLLLLLLLLLLLLLLL
OOOOOOOOOOOOOOOOOOOOOOOOO
LLLLLLLLLLLLLLLLLLLLLLLLLLLLLLLL

...reading what I wrote makes me laugh at my precedent naivety.

If only it were that simple. It is not my goal here to try and define love for you. I think we all shape our own definitions of love based on our experiences. This book explores my own experiences which instigated how I define love. I can't define love for you.

Of course, this book wouldn't be worth reading if I just blatantly told you my definition of love. There are hundreds of books which explain love in similar ways I explain it in. It's not what this is about. This is about showing you my journey, and letting you ***experience*** how I came to my definition of love.

This is a story interwoven with real-life, reflective journal entries which observe a journey of discovering self, and in return discovering love.

What I didn't anticipate was how much I learned about myself in writing this book. In essence, this book is about how I found me. But deeper still, it required a willingness to be honest with myself in your presence.

First Draft:

I can paint a self-portrait for you,
But when I show you who I am
everything may not be as it's pictured.
I can paint handsome over these scars
the tone of my melanin,
the hue of my eyes,
it's beautiful art
aesthetically pleasing and valued
a painting exactly as I hope you pictured it
within your frame of mind.

But I've spent too much time behind this mask.
I'm beginning to paint these flaws,
see how I painted the imprint of my disguise
traced along my jawline,
my complexion contrast is different there
exposing my bruised brow,

darkly colored flesh behind these ears
to extenuate the numb
from these strappings.

So I don't know how I'll feel
if when I show you who I am,
you tell me I'm strapping,
'cause I know my handsome leaves scars.
My melanin skin,
the same hue as my eyes,
the reflection of my dark soul.
I am beautiful, dark art
abstract and priceless,

I'm just an artist.

<u>Second Draft:</u>

I can paint a self-portrait for you,
~~*but when I show you who I am*~~
~~*everything may not be as it's pictured.*~~
~~*I can paint handsome over these scars*~~
~~*the tone of my melanin,*~~
~~*the hue of my eyes,*~~
~~*it's beautiful art*~~
~~*aesthetically pleasing and valued*~~
~~*a painting exactly as I hope you pictured it*~~
~~*within your frame of mind.*~~

But I've spent too much time behind this mask.
~~*I'm beginning to paint these flaws,*~~
~~*see how I painted the imprint of my disguise*~~
~~*traced along my jawline,*~~

~~my complexion contrast is different there~~
~~exposing my bruised brow,~~
~~darkly colored flesh behind these ears~~
~~to extenuate the numb~~
~~from these strappings.~~

So I don't know how I'll ~~feel~~
~~if when I~~ show you who I am,
~~you tell me I'm strapping,~~

Cause I know my handsome leaves scars
~~my melanin skin~~
~~the same hue as my eyes,~~
~~the reflection of my dark soul.~~
I am beautiful, dark art
abstract and priceless,

I'm just an artist.

<u>Final Draft:</u>

~~I can paint~~ A self-portrait for you,
~~But when I show you who I am~~
~~everything may not be as it's pictured.~~
~~I can paint handsome over these scars~~
~~the tone of my melanin,~~
~~the hue of my eyes,~~
~~it's beautiful art~~
~~aesthetically pleasing and valued~~
~~a painting exactly as I hope you pictured it~~
~~within your frame of mind.~~

~~But I've spent too much time~~ behind this mask.

About Her

~~I'm beginning to paint these flaws,~~
~~see how I painted the imprint of my disguise~~
~~traced along my jawline,~~
~~my complexion contrast is different there~~
~~exposing my bruised brow,~~
~~darkly colored flesh behind these ears~~
~~to extenuate the numb~~
~~from these strappings.~~

~~So I don't know how~~ I'll ~~feel~~
~~if when I~~ show you who I am,
~~you tell me I'm strapping,~~
~~'cause I know~~ my handsome ~~leaves~~ scars.
~~my melanin skin,~~
~~the same hue as my eyes,~~
~~the reflection of my dark soul.~~
I am ~~beautiful, dark art~~
~~abstract and priceless,~~

I'm ~~just~~ an artist.

1

GOD IN HER

November 29, 2020

How do I define what a woman means to me apart from the physical being? Does the definition come to me naturally? Is it already etched in my consciousness at birth, just waiting to be discovered? What if I never discover it? Are all of my thoughts purely learned behavior, or are there energies beyond the threshold of my physical self, instigating how I think about women?

It's probably important to set the foundation of what "HER" means to me. Moving forward through this story I'm going to share with you, this will serve as the definition of HER.

HER, here, refers to feminine energy. That's it. A being

with an over-abundance of feminine energy in comparison to masculine energy; This is what I consider HER. I leave it to you to decide what that looks like physically. I have my preferences, but they have no relevance to what I'm about to tell you.

This leads us back to my original question. If one disregards the biology of it all, how do we define “HER?” Feminine energy? So, what is feminine energy?

My best definition of "feminine energy" is from a blog I once read while doing research on meditation. It was written by Rena Satre Meloy. She discussed "Balancing Our Feminine and Masculine Energy."

Rena describes feminine energy as the "being" mode of human behavior, highlighted by a receiving heart, an intuitive mind, and a focus on the internal self as opposed to the external. This is further characterized by high levels of emotion, receptivity, fluidity, empathy, vulnerability, creativity, and an instinct to be nurturing. By contrast, masculine energy is the "doing" mode of human behavior highlighted by a giving heart, a logical mind, and a focus on the external. This is further characterized by high levels of projectivity, focus on goals and achievement, tenacity, and an instinct to be sheltering.

Before you go down the winding path of what "HER” means to you, let's stay on point. **This is how I define “HER.”** I will add some context by saying, I believe we all are inherently composed of both masculine and feminine energy. It's just a matter of which spirit is stronger within us. How you choose to make a connection to gender roles or societal norms is none of my concern. What is important here is how we foster our relationships based on how we define what “HER” means. This is what it means to me and how it is referenced in this story.

I can confidently say, how I define "HER" is a combination of learned behavior and self discovery. It often times brings me to a point of contradiction where I am forced to redefine my understanding (or lack thereof.) This is however, the case for all understanding, an ocean of barely scratched surfaces...

I call her Queen, because I recognize her excellence and how she loves both herself and her people equally.
I call her Queen because of her ambition, her love, her creativity, and her empathetic mentality.
I call her Queen because she is what inspires me emotionally and spiritually.
I call her Queen because she is the provider of my opportunities.
I call her Queen because she exemplifies strength through femininity.
I call her Queen because she led me to be the King I was destined to be.

You were Mother Earth before I became Atom,
nurtured by your roots
and shaped by the cosmic waves of this energy they call love.
You were Mother before I knew your name,
Mom before I could ever understand how peace transcends through pain,
heavenly love expressed on this earthly plane.
You were Mother before I would ever love another,

my first love until my last breath,
the only woman I've feared with a Godlike respect,
my She-Ra, my Isis, it's me you fought to protect.
The King I am, you saw, before I ever noticed him.
You knew who I was destined to be,
introduced the feminine to my masculine,
so I too, would know how to love and be love,
unconditionally.

How could ***she*** *come from* ***his*** *rib*
when it is through her,
I live.
Formed in the likeness of God from birth,
molded and nurtured by her here on earth,
she is love,
so is she God?
Is God she?
She, like God,
loves unconditionally,
or God, like she,
loves without conditions,
loves me,
despite my flaws,
my guilt,
my lies,
my falls,
how selfish of me,
to so intimately receive her love,
without ever understanding her pain.

How could God feel pain?
She forgives.
She just always seems to know.
She feels me.
She sees me.
She hears me.
Our connection extends beyond umbilical cords.
She's always with me,
like God.

I WAS RAISED by two Moms. I mean it literally... just not simultaneously. Probably like most of you, I didn't grow up in a nuclear family. Mine was more of a nuclear explosion. But, at the core of it all, we were still family. Sidebar: Did you know only about 18% of US households are considered 'nuclear families'? I mean even at its highest in the 70's, it was still only around 40%. I'm not a sociologist or an anthropologist, so don't quote me on it, but most of us did not grow up within this type of social construct and yet society maintains it as "the way." Maybe it is, who knows? One thing is for sure, it certainly isn't the only way. Shit... I think I turned out just fine.

SHE IS EARTH.
God is She.
The Portal.
From Spiritual
to Physical,
Emotional Being.
She is Love
Unconditionally.
She is the Bearer

of Heavenly Beings,
the Carrier of Creation,
the Creator's Queen.
She is Existence,
the Manifestation of Beauty,
Look close at her Femininity.
You will see the makings of men,
Divine, the yang to my Masculine.
She is many things, most namely
Everything.

I GREW up with my first mom until I was about eight or so. Then I spent the rest of my childhood with my second mom. The irony of this story is my father had very little to do with either phase, in regards to raising me, I mean. I really wanted to avoid this topic, but it would be confusing to leave it out of context. Context which is probably important in understanding how I came to define "**HER**" in the way I do.

Strong woman, black woman, understandably
misunderstood woman,
been called out your name, but you still show love
woman,
and I love you woman, will always call you my
own woman.
You're my air woman, my breath of life woman,
I inhale you when I'm feeling down so I can get
high,
rise above this cold world and let it pass me by.
I inhale you when shit gets hard,
'cause your high eases my mind woman.

Your breath is the wind beneath my wings
carrying me to higher elevations,
blowing my mind and filling me with inspi-
rations,
molding me with aspirations.
I may be disguised with his reflection,
but it's you on the inside that oxidized this
creation.
What I mean is,
You're my air woman,
my breath of life woman,
I inhale you and become reminiscent of time
spent being in your presence,
when hard headedness made me a victim of ill
punishment.
Yet and still the beholder of your comfort,
and many days I find myself looking forward to
yesterday, like it was tomorrow.
So I'll inhale you deep today, before I find myself
exhaling you in sorrow.

Strong woman,
black woman,
understandably misunderstood woman,
been called out your name but always showed
love woman.

As I was saying, the first eight years of my life I lived with my first mom. I won't be using the terms biological mom or step-mom here. To me they are both equally my mom and I don't hold one in a higher regard than the other. I have no recollection of my father while living with my first mom. Well, that's not completely true. I remember how he used to make my mom cry all the time. Mostly because he just wasn't there to help her or to at least pick us up, sometimes. Yes... us.

My sister. Have I mentioned her? My little sister, Colleen... or Cauliflower. It was me, Cauliflower, and Jason. Jason had a different Dad and only lived with us for a year. However, Mom would drag us out to West Philly every chance she got to spend time with Jay.

Within the actual household it was just me, my mom, and Cauliflower. We moved a number of times, sometimes with family, mostly to small apartments around North Philly. I didn't talk much. I was super introverted and I loved my mom very intimately. Not in a weird way, but I remember always thinking how beautiful she was and always looking forward to her coming home from work. So, yeah, single mom of three, pretty destitute, maybe a little dysfunctional, but all in all, I remember being happy with HER. I felt loved... until she broke my heart.

I loved her the best way I knew how,
without the need to know why.
It just was,
without stimulus or conditions,
it just was.
Her being was enough,
I associated her presence with God's gift
her vibe with my favorite lyric,
her hug was an out of body experience.
I loved her in a way that didn't require me to
understand it,
it just was.
Until it wasn't,
my love left with her when we departed

or it fell into the fault line of a broken heart
I didn't even know existed.

At around eight or so I vaguely remember my mom asking me if I wanted to visit my Dad: key word, visit. Who knew a visit would last a lifetime. Now, as an adult, I can understand her reasoning, but then, I felt betrayed. I don't think if I knew I would never be coming home, I would have wanted to go. Then again, I don't know if she even knew what we were getting into. Either way, I was a child, and my feelings were my feelings regardless of her intention.

Sometimes, our parents teach us things they don't even know they are teaching us. During the time, I learned how to turn off my feelings. I wouldn't let anyone else get close. Besides, I was already an introvert, so it was easy to just bottle everything up and go unnoticed.

Keep in mind, I was a child and I'm writing from a reflective state of being. None of this was intentional. My subconscious was simply applying a tourniquet to stop the internal bleeding. But you know what happens when you leave a tourniquet on for too long? Everything begins to go numb.

My second mom, was now in the picture. My dad was, too. He was a provider for sure. He worked more than anything. I never thought of him as a protector, or someone I could talk to, or anything like that. It was ironic to be living with my dad, but not ever seeing him. Having him there, but not having him.

The 1st time I hugged my father
I was at my high school graduation.
I was damn near a man.
The little boy in me wanted to hold on

despite awkwardly feeling like
I was hugging a stranger,
which was ironic as I was always known as
my father's doppelgänger.
My mother saw me.
I could see the faint hint of disdain
in the tint of her eyes,
her pain saw him.
So when I heard shit like...
look at you, chip off the old block, ain'tcha?
that shit left a chip on my shoulder.

I liked him.
I just didn't want to be like him.
A reflection cast in
broken mirrors
shattered by a rolling stone.
If he couldn't see himself clear enough
to recognize God within himself,
how could he possibly see me?
Maybe he saw me as his reckoning
without realizing I was his blessing,
his 2nd chance to be a better man.

I remember not remembering him.
but recall seeing his chess moves.
Heartless,
leaving me like a sacrificed piece in this manipulative game.
He played to maintain control of his own peace.
My father taught me how to play chess
and I focused on how he was moving,
so I wouldn't become him.

The type of man who uses queens as pawns.
If he would've just taken those
Knights to focus on me,
or teach me how to take an L
and turn it into my best move,
maybe help me realize how to move as a
Blackman in white spaces.
He captured my heart,
but took a rain-check on teaching me how to reign
as a King.
I taught that to myself
in this game of life,
and I say that proudly with my whole "chest."

I've since learned to appreciate our long distance
relationship,
grown-ass me, still looking forward to his call,
6-year-old me, wondering if the notification
sound
could possibly be him,
until 7-year-old me chimes in
to talk me off the ledge and back
behind this flood wall we built
to protect us from a wave of expectations
I saw in my mother's face so many times.
The river she cried.
Same river where I learned
it's either
sink or swim.
down in the deep end of rejection,
damn near drowning,
but I inhaled and held a deep
breath of inflated emotion to keep

my head above water,
doggie paddling,
until I became sure of myself.

I tried to forget,
but the receding floods
left a watermark on my heart.
It reminds me
how nice it would have been
to have been picked by him,
or to have him pick me up and dry me off under
the sun.
To have him "raisin" me,
instead of me just being a raisin in the sun.
Like a dream deferred,
maybe I wouldn't have felt like
Langston Hughes with an attitude,
Or so much like a man with something to prove.

I allowed the chip to grow boulder,
until it felt like I was bearing
the weight of the world on my shoulders.
I "Atlas" realized,
I had to let go,
and let it roll off
by forgiving him.
That's when this chip off the old block
became the cornerstone
of the building blocks
to this skyscraper of a man.
but never tall enough
to eclipse the light of being a sun,
so no shade Pops...

it's all love.

My second mom had children of her own, but for the sake of staying on topic I don't want to take a deep dive here. The short story is, my dad ended up leaving and I stayed with my second mom. My sister moved back in with my first mom. Then there was my second sister, who was my second mom's first daughter, and my third sister, who was my second mom's younger best friend. I had a fourth sister, too. She was my dad's second daughter. She was a queen he managed to place on the board in the manipulative game of chess I mentioned earlier. I didn't know her very well. Stick with me, I'm trying to paint a picture here. There was also my second and third brother, both from my second mom. They were both a lot older than me, and I didn't really spend much time with them. Do you see where I'm going with this? The moral of this short story is part of my life has been largely defined by my interactions with motherly and sisterly energy. It was how I learned a large portion of my life lessons.

In my eyes, my second mother was the epitome of a strong black woman. She was a caretaker, a hustler, a provider, a protector. She was my everything. For a long time I resisted loving her the way I loved my first mom. I ended up winning the battle, because I didn't love her the way I loved my first mom; I loved her differently. We expressed love differently to one another, as she had a hard outer shell. She taught me to have one, too. She was the one who toughened me up. She made sure my masculinity stayed in tact. Nowadays some would call it toxic, but it was far from it. She was exactly what I needed at the time. Of course, at the time, I thought she was just mean, but even then, I found comfort in her scolding. Maybe because I knew she was paying attention to me.

Her figure was hidden beneath aprons and a
black dress,
stained with the breast milk dripping from the
privileged lips of masculine pride,
her worth compressed in an outer shell of black
coal hiding the diamond inside.
Her figure was hidden beneath white scrubs
stained with the blood of male egos and the
tears of the chauvinist who couldn't bear the
pain of the rib being pulled from his side,
exposing the hidden truth: she was not bore from
him, she was him.
The shield which protected each breath and heart
beat,
the Achilles of his stride,
as he would fall without her.
Her figure was hidden behind dishpan hands,
and her voice muffled by baby cries,
her perfection overlooked, as she stood watch over
the legacy of family trees,
planting and nurturing seeds,
her thumbs turned green and sore,
she lost grip of the reality of who she was destined
to be.
Her figure was hidden where all could see,
as the shape of her mother nature was the silhou-
ette of the Universe.
The true image of a God who gives life and
nurtures souls,
whose energy quenches man's thirst:

thirst to exist, to be, to become,
to become one with God by acknowledging her
presence.
Her figure was only hidden in the eyes of
mortal men,
who can not recognize the God within,
she would raise Kings who recognized Queens
enhance their state of being to be elevated
amongst men.

2

THE THREE SISTERS

December 3, 2020

Today I read about the Three Sisters. Apparently corn, beans, and squash were known as the Three Sisters by the Cherokee and Iroquois. They interplanted these crops in a unique system where each crop played a role in the nurturing and development of the other. First was the corn, which was planted on a small hill. Then came the beans, which were planted after the corn, but in the same area. Last came the squash, which was planted in between the rows of corn and beans. The stalk of the corn served as a pillar for the beans to wrap around. Beans supplied nitrates and fertilized the soil and the leaves of the squash protected the soil from weeds. They grew better together. I was always closer with my sisters than my brothers, so *perhaps I was cultivated somewhere in the garden with them.*

Renee would have definitely been the corn. She has always been a pillar in my life, plus she was the oldest. We may not share the same roots but she has always nurtured me emotionally. I've always admired her, as she was the toughest of the bunch. If "keep it real" were a person, it would be her.

She is the one person in the world I've never wanted to disappoint. If I ever did, you can be certain she would be sure to let me know. Her tongue was sharp. She'd cut you deep and mend your wounds at the same time. She taught me to be a fighter. I was always very calm and collected, but I learned the difference between being nice and being kind from her. To be honest, there were a few fights I got into solely because I knew if I didn't, I was going to have to hear her mouth when she found out I let shit slide.

Between her and my second mom, I'd take an L in a fight any day. I'm laughing, and also, I'm dead serious. Even to this day, I don't want to disappoint her.

Always be kind
sometimes be nice
just never forget,
being kind
is not always nice.

Wanda would be the beans. Like Renee, we didn't share the same roots. You know, the one sibling who was always in trouble? That was Wanda. I think one time she stacked up like ninety consecutive days of punishment time. If "gave no fucks" was a person, it was her. I never saw a person repeatedly do the same thing over and over, just to get caught 90% of the time. But she was a gambler, 'cause she would roll the dice every time.

Wanda was older than me as well. She was a fighter, too. I remember we got in a fight one time and she swears she whopped my ass. If she tells you, don't believe it. She did toss me on one occasion, though. Let me explain.

Wanda was bigger than me: taller and thicker. It wasn't uncommon for the heat to not be working in the house, and sometimes it would be pretty cold. One morning, I was trying to squeeze in a few more minutes before getting out of bed. Her ass came into my room and snatched the covers off of me. The frigid air pinched my skin and shocked my soul. I jumped out of bed in my tighty-whities and ran straight into her room.

In that split second, I didn't know what I was going to do. If I threw hands, Ma Dukes would be on my ass, and I didn't want those problems. Plus, my skinny ass definitely couldn't wrestle her and get the win. I quickly realized the error in my ways. But it was too late, she had already laid hands on me and with a grunt like one from a wildebeest, she shoved me out of her room. I learned to fly that day, catching some air before it was knocked out of me, as I slammed into the hallway closet door. I jumped up and said some silly shit like, "Try that shit again and see what happens! You play too damn much!!" Unless I absolutely had to protect myself, I could never hit a woman and she knew that shit. She took advantage of the situation.

Wanda had my back, though. She whopped a few asses in middle school for me when I found myself in a predicament with some hood rat who wanted to get beside herself.

So, fertilizer. Wanda was very sexually active. When I

moved in with my second mom, I didn't really know about sex. I don't have a problem admitting it now, but at a young age, I was molested by a family member. I kept it to myself... there wasn't anyone for me to tell. I never went to therapy for it either, we just didn't go to therapy back then. But, I still didn't know anything about sex.

Wanda would always sneak guys over when my mom wasn't home and she was left in charge of us. There were times I saw more than I probably should have. Other times, I learned by way of her friends.

Remember, Wanda was older than me, which means her friends were older than me as well, and I was always the "cute little brother." I think you can see where I'm going with this. My true introduction to sex was through a few of them. By the time I was thirteen, I had already had sexual experiences most eighteen years olds only experienced by way of their father's hidden stash of porn. I kept it all to myself, but secretly wore it like a badge of honor. This is why I say Wanda was the beans. By being around her, I indirectly learned about the fertilization process.

She said she would make me a man
coated me with her secret serum
told me it would harden me
make me tough
but her kiss, rabid,
turned me savage
or addict
the way I craved to be more man
or beast
or fiend for her wetness.

And then there was Colleen, commonly known as

Cauliflower. I don't remember who gave her the nickname, but it stuck. She was, and is, a flower: elegant, feminine, sleek, innocent, sophisticated, but still bore the thorns of a rose. So yes, Cauliflower, instead of squash. She still served the same purpose, though. She protected the soil from the weeds with her leaves.

I loved my little sister immensely. We had the same roots. Honestly, I should have been the one protecting her. I was never an overbearing protector. Growing up the way I did taught me the importance of learning to fight your own battles. Sometimes I do wish I had fought more battles for her, maybe she wouldn't have had to deal with some of the things I did. But hell, I didn't even know how to protect myself. I don't mean physically. I could definitely throw hands, if I had to. Where I was from, it was a non-negotiable. What I mean is emotionally. I was just a child though, so I don't beat myself up about it too much.

Physically, she didn't really need my protecting anyways. I remember one of my girlfriends kept messing with her. I don't remember why, but my girl kept talking shit, poking the bear. In the blink of an eye, Colleen was on her ass like bees on honey. It looked like there were about twenty fists flying, all of them Colleen's and all of them connecting. My girl was caught so off guard, she could only try to hold on for dear life. Colleen pinned her up against a wall.

It happened so fast, no one really knew how to react. Renee started laughing and everyone else kind of just stood there in shock for a few seconds before breaking it up. It was awkward for me. My little sister had just beat the brakes off my girlfriend and my girlfriend had started it. I could only stand there with shoulders shrugged, hands out, mouth wide open, with a "what am I supposed to do?" face.

Despite the girlfriend incident, and the time she

dropped a flying elbow in my back, which got her banned from watching female wrestling on TV and left me screaming in pain, she wasn't really a fighter. Her spirit was consoling. I always knew she'd do anything for me. I don't think there is anything I've asked her for she has complained about doing or hesitated to do. Even to this day.

Sister,
don't stand behind me
I need you to stand beside me
let them see you
and know if I do stand in front of you
it's because I need them to see
what they must go through
should they ever try to bring harm to you.

3

JEZEBEL

In high school, I had my share of girlfriends, but there was one in particular who really had an impact on me. Out of everyone else she was different.

I saw her without realizing
I had lost my own vision
looking to love someone else
before I learned to find love in myself
left me blindsided when she left me
like leftovers in a doggie bag
I was left holding
in the middle of left field
wondering where it all went left
and maybe it left a mark
but all these lefts
got me right back to the start
Now I'm left to decide
between falling in love again
or never falling
and I chose the "latter"

to get over my first love.

March 24, 2021

Today I read a story about Jezebel. I have always remembered the name from the Bible, I believe in the book of Kings. I simply thought Jezebel just referred to an immoral woman who would shamelessly do whatever she needed to get whatever she wanted. As it turns out, it's much deeper than that. Jezebel was the wife of King Ahab, who ruled the kingdom of Israel.

When Jezebel married Ahab, she basically persuaded him to believe in other gods. Infer from it what you wish, but she legit convinced this man to change his religion. Jezebel didn't play games either. Anyone who stood in her way found themselves on the receiving end of her wrath. It didn't matter who you were, either. From common folk, to the prophets of the land at the time, she would have you killed. You may have heard of Elijah from the Bible, well, she even sent him packing, running for his life. Long story short, this eventually lead to a civil war in Israel. She ended up being thrown out of a window and eaten by dogs, or something like that.

Yeah, pretty horrific story. Now that I

think about it, I definitely know a Jezebel! Well my Jezebel wasn't as bad as the real Jezebel, but she was pretty bad. In her defense, knowing what I know now, I believe she had been abused early on in life and she was just a product of her environment.

She's in a deep sleep
laid in a pole position
dreamin' of fast cash and fast cars
pinches don't wake her
only leave her soul scared
'cause she done went too far
she over par
trying to get a hole in one-or-two shots
getting tipsy to make the body rock
in the champagne room
she making them corks pop
and they got many 1's
so now they pockets got 2 knots
and they both for her
and they love to watch
from the VIP skybox
they see she batting balls
stage name Chicago White Soxs
so they pitch the game
it's money
she stuck playing sweet sexy
call her Honey
5'6" caramel skin body right
thick ass

nice breasts, waist tight
I mean she got these negus weak
call her kryptonite
'cause they giving up they green
to gain the strength to defeat her self esteem
she claims to be standing on her own two feet
like we don't see the pole she using to lean
she dignifies her actions
as a ways and means
not realizing she the onlyfan
she ever really needs
she playing the role of porn star
but believes she's an actress
allowing social media to direct the scene
now she addicted to the dopamine
behind the scenes
somebody re-write the script
our daughters is watching
and this chick way past PG-13
it's time for the final episode
to her, her ass is her biggest asset
but it's acid
we watching her soul erode
she a sleeping beauty
eyes wide open, can't see the reel
she don't even understand
the meaning of a women no more
she defines her womanhood
through her sex appeal
She has submitted and become a slave to the bills
and they got those
but no bouquet for her
just a rose signed

with a card for the hoes
so shake that ass, momma
make that cash, momma
you can always afford
to take your spirit back
but you got too much baggage
hidden behind your conscience
and tucked with your pride
she never finds herself beautiful enough
because she's lost on the inside
She in a deep sleep
laid in a pole position
dreaming a nightmare
but 'aint Prince coming to wake her
she be Maleficent...
lost in the woods somewhere.

I really don't even want to get into the particulars of our relationship, 'cause man was I stupid. But she was my first love. I can say it honestly and know I mean it. It was probably the most toxic relationship I've ever been in to date. I'm lying. It was the most toxic relationship I was ever in, **PERIOD.** We met through family, and it felt like our family supported the shenanigans. I'll give you one story, but just know there are many.

Jezebel used to live on the edge of the city with my sister, my second mom's third daughter. She was my sister's husband's cousin. Now the apartments she stayed in were not the projects, but a lot of the folks who lived there definitely had hood mentality. There was a group of dudes who used to live right where Jezebel did, and whenever I went over, they would be outside. There was never any beef or anything, but we weren't cool either. We just stayed out of each other's way. On this particular day, it was me, my cousin, and Jezebel. I wasn't supposed to be there because no adults were home, so I ended up jus' chillin' for a second and then leaving. When I left of course the Wannabee Thugs Gang was outside. When I walked by, the energy felt weird because one of them spoke to me. We would speak from time to time, but this particular time, it was overly friendly. I shrugged it off and headed home.

Once I got home, something just told me to go back over there. Plus, honestly, I figured I could get some right quick before anyone got home. So I headed back over. The apartment was only like a fifteen minute walk or five minute bike ride. I can't remember if I walked or took my bike. In any case I got back over there and my cousin was sitting outside. When she saw me, her jaw damn near hit the bottom step of the little stoop she was sitting on. I remember her exact words were, "Welp, I'm goin' to take a walk!" And just like that, she got up and left. I thought it was weird, and my spidey senses were going off.

I went in the house and it was dead silent. I walked up to Jezebel's door and knocked... no answer. I knocked again... no answer. I tried to open the door. It was unlocked, but something was pressed up against it, so I couldn't get in. I called her name. She told me to hold on, she was sleeping. The bed was up against the back side of the door. I forced the door open and she was standing there.

Her hair was a mess. She definitely had been in bed, but she hadn't been sleeping. I could tell by the sheets all over the place and the used condom next to the pillow. I acted like I didn't see it. She tried to tell me she was taking a nap, but the tears were already welling up in her eyes. I don't even think she was able to get the lie all the way out. I pushed the bed back to its normal position, casually. Really,

I wanted to see if someone was under the bed. No one was there. Which meant only one thing. He had to be in the closet. There was nowhere else to go. I mean, he could have gone out the window. I had snuck in and out of the window plenty of times, but everything happened so fast, I doubted they would've had time to get the window open, remove the screen and put everything back. So I knew he was in the closet.

I opened the closet door and, of course, he was standing there. Here is the funny part. I thought we were about to fight and I was ready. However, I tell you, this dude turned into the biggest bitch I'd ever seen. He was legit scared. He kept saying, "I didn't know! She told me you were her cousin!" He just kept repeating it. I wanted to hit him, but honestly, I believed him.

I wanted to hit her, but I knew better than that. At this point, he had stepped out of the closet and was standing besides the large mirror, which was attached to her dresser. I looked up at him and I could see him, me, and Jezebel, the latter two as reflections. Up until this point, I had kept my cool, but the instant I saw our reflections, I snapped. I hit the mirror with my fist and the unit completely detached from the dresser. It slammed against the wall. Jezebel screamed and the dude, I can't recall his name, ran out of the apartment.

By this time, my cousin had come back. She must've heard the commotion. I casually walked outside, showing no emotion, and went back home. Thinking about it now, I'm pretty sure I had my bike. It wasn't until I got back home I realized the blood. My hand was busted up pretty bad. My mom asked me what happened and I told her. She told me she was disappointed in me. It stung more than my hand. I had to go get stitches.

When I got back, my mom, my sister, and Jezebel were at the house. My mom told me I needed to sit down and talk to Jezebel about what had happened. I wanted to tell her "HELL NO!" but I knew better.

First of all, I probably would have ended up with more stitches, and secondly, my mom always made me face my problems. She made me face my issues and fight if I had to, even if I got my ass beat. It's just what it was. My sister was in the background complaining about the broken mirror. I don't remember what I said to Jezebel, or if I even said anything at all. I was just following orders. I remember thinking, "How in the fuck did I become the bad guy in this?" Everyone was mad at me. At the time, I didn't understand. I was so broken on the inside, but I didn't shed a tear, not one. This was my fault. I had let someone else in. And I shouldn't have done it. Especially not Jezebel.

If all is fair in love and war,
then why does love always leave scars?
Scars that can never leave.

I didn't fall in love easy
but when I did, I fell hard
and it broke my heart.

Like I said, just one of the many stories in regards to my relationship with Jezebel. I decided to call her Jezebel because looking back on it, I can see how she changed me as a person. I wasn't hanging out with my friends anymore. I stopped doing well in school. I started smoking. Figuratively speaking, she had persuaded me to change how I worshipped God. Hence... Jezebel.

She said, "I'm available,"
but I thought she said,
"I'm in love with you."
Lust must've slipped
oxytocin in my cup.

I didn't understand why the women I loved the most were always so upset with me when it came to Jezebel, but I know now. It was because they expected more from me. However, they were not going to step in and force my hand. They needed me to learn how to man the fuck up and handle my shit. I didn't know it, though. Just like they didn't know how broken I was.

As a young boy
I was never taught how
to deal with my own emotions
I only knew how to cry in the dark
to air them out
any change in my atmosphere
would cause the water to rise in my eyes
and flood my senses with insecurity
but only bitch ass negus cry
and Momma said, "Ain't no sissies in my house."
Threats dried my eyes,
but she never understood what my tears were
about,
she ignored the warnings,
she couldn't see it was these
unchecked emotions
causing an internal global warming.

As a teenager,

I tried to keep it cool under these ice caps,
but I was hotheaded
I thought it would keep me grounded
but real negus don't let shit fly.
The haze of an unfiltered sun was
blurring my vision
I knew Momma would be proud
My red flags looked like victory streamers
imagine my surprise
when she told me my temperament
gave her chills.

As a young man,
I was told I could be cold hearted.
I lacked emotion.
It seemed as if I just couldn't "wind"
even with these turbines
built by therapy sessions
designed to cool my temperament
channel my chi
disperse positive energy
blow off some steam
get me somewhere between this hot head
and a cold heart
lukewarm
but I just felt stuck
frozen in position behind icy walls
buried in a snowfall
where I could hibernate my
vulnerabilities
there in the frigid air
if my tongue dare speaks on them
it stuck and turned numb

so I kept it all bottled in
self-regulation turned my heart cold
but my blood still boiled
eventually it would expand and explode.

Maybe if I was able to understand what they were trying to teach me, my life and my understanding of HER would have taken a completely different trajectory. Maybe I would have landed on Venus and learned how to breathe in her atmosphere. Instead I landed on Mars. Maybe it was exactly where I needed to be.

I didn't need to put my energy into forgetting you,
I just channeled my chi to remember me.

4

LOSING SIGHT OF HER

I would join the Army straight out of high school. Literally two weeks after I graduated, I was headed to Fort Jackson, Mississippi to Basic Training. Just a few months prior, I had actually intended to go to college.

I was a high school athlete, decent at football, good at track, and full of potential. I signed up to be in the Army my junior year of high school through a delayed entry program. I decided not to take the SATs or the ACT test. My track coach was furious! He arranged a meeting with the track coach from LaSalle University in Philly, and I was scheduled to take the ACT test paid for by him. He wanted me to go to his school to run track. I was excited.

When I got home from school, I was even more excited to tell my mom about it. As I was explaining the details of what had transpired with the coach from Lasalle, I saw her body language shift, as if she was irritated. She had this way of holding her cigarette and glaring at you above her glasses. It let you know she was not impressed. By the time I finished explaining, I felt like I was defending myself, as opposed to sharing exciting news. I really didn't understand what was wrong. She puffed her cigarette. I swear she hadn't blinked the whole time. She said, "You know, I was really looking forward to you getting up out my house. Who you think is paying for you to go to school?"

She hadn't heard a word I said. beyond the fact I was reconsidering going to the Army for school. I hadn't heard a word she said beyond, "I was really looking forward to you getting up out my house."

As I mentioned before, our relationship wasn't one which exhibited a lot of emotion, but up until this point, I never knew she felt this way. Truth was, I had no idea how she felt at all. The statement would forever change the course of my life. Whether she said it consciously or not, it changed me. It hurt. It hurt bad. Despite how it made me feel, I knew it was time for me to become a man.

She was tired of watching me
and knowing what to expect from me
her eyes were heavy with expectations of me
I couldn't see.

She was tired of watching me
And I never realized she saw me
until I felt her stop staring.

She was tired of watching me
so she closed her eyes
to ask God to watch over me
she prayed for me
hoping I would see what she saw in me.

I was 18 years old and on my own, literally. I could do whatever the fuck I wanted and no one could tell me shit (minus the fact I was in the Army.) I had a "girlfriend" at the time, but truth was I was all over the place. I didn't even trust her. I had caught her cheating on me once already.

I didn't really have much faith in relationships at this point, but I still considered myself a gentlemen. I told myself I would always treat women respectfully. In my world, I did, but in reality, I had no damn clue what I was doing. I had no clue what love meant to me. I had mistaken chivalry with respect. Over the next couple of years, I would have quite a few sexual partners and empty relationships. I won't say all of these relationships were meaningless, though. They were learning experiences.

I was addicted.
Lust was the placebo
Love prescribed
to deal with the pain of heartbreak,
I felt the withdrawal
when the prescription ran out
I felt the agony of facing the real.

~

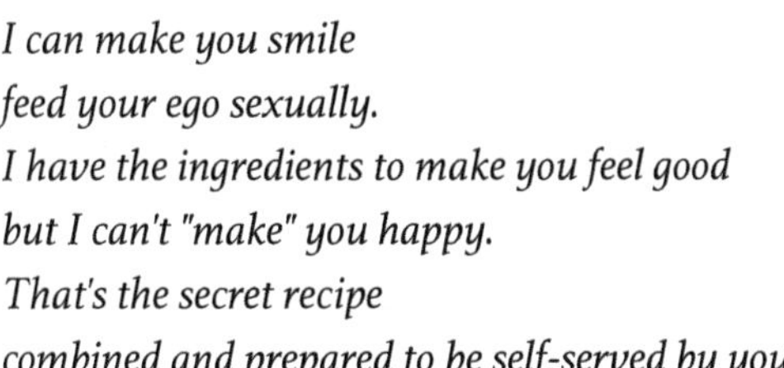

I can make you smile
feed your ego sexually.
I have the ingredients to make you feel good
but I can't "make" you happy.
That's the secret recipe
combined and prepared to be self-served by you.

~

I want to learn to breathe
under the surface of you.
so I can raise my fin
separate your body of water
and get drenched in you.
Dive in and swim deep into sin with you
explore the depths of you
where it's hard to handle the pressure.
I want to steal your treasure
ocean eleven with you.
I want to breathe you in
and exhale what's left of you
so I won't drown myself
in the pleasure of you.

Take me at face value.
Don't buy into the abstract of me
at your silent auction,
expecting to get change.
I'm showing you my worth
autographed with my pseudonym name.
Either you take me as is
or make a bid for a body of work
to better accentuate your space.
I'm worth a pretty penny,
but the only change you'll see in me
that makes "cents"
is the change I want to create.

Someone told me once
we breathe 18 breaths a minute.
6-6-6
fillin' me with devilish intent
as if this were last breath.
I'll make it well spent.
I'll put my nose to the scent of your memory
inhale you deep
until you exhale ecstasy
exclaimed in erotic echoes
from the depth of my erection
which erodes erroneous engagements
engraved, etched in our ego
by imitations of an orgasm.
I'll sex you well
like your man's supposed to
touch you like your body wants me to
leave you gasping
grabbing your chest
begging for another breath
of me.

Let me be your poem.
Get your body to rhyme
in the same stanza as mine
be your haiku:

the-voice-that-you-hear
the-vibe-you-feel-will-let-me
o-pen-mic-night-you

Give you a free verse of how I really feel
make your fingers snap
watch your inhibitions disappear
run it back
make your fingers snap
watch your wet appear
it's the me in the metaphor
the lic in this lyric of mine
giving imagery of you
opening your book
for me behind closed doors.

5

SHEBA

July, 14, 2021

I read about the Queen of Sheba today. She was a character in the movie "Three Thousand Years of Longing," which was actually a decent movie in my opinion. It lead me to want to get her back story.

The story of the Queen of Sheba is a debated legend. It has been elaborated upon throughout Asia and Africa, especially in Jewish, Islamic, Yemenite and Ethiopian traditions. Some scholars debate her existence.

In the Ethiopian Tradition, the queen is known as Makeda, a faithful and determined leader. Makeda rose to power to prevent chaos from prevailing. She stepped into her role and restored security and stability to her land.

When I met her, she told me her nickname was Sheba. Said her mother called her that. I had heard of the Queen of Sheba before, but had never heard the story behind the name. I doubt if she ever did either. I believe to her, it just sounded regal. I would find out soon enough, the name did in fact suit her well.

There I was waiting on route 4
to move me into a new season
and I saw her
skin reflecting the hue of an autumn sunset
moving in my direction.

Who knew she would be
the fall of my spiritual insurrection.
Initially I saw her in body
but when we made eye contact
I recognized what she embodied.

When I spoke to her, I respected her.
I caressed her with my words.
She was receptive
and stroked me back with hers.
I paid close attention
to see where the beauty lies.
She listened with intent
silently reading between my lines.

We got lost in one another
absorbing each others aura
until route 4 came
opening the door for us
we rode the bus

enjoying presence and conversation
both missed our stops
but found our destination.

I'm attracted to her greatness
turned on by the power of her confidence
infatuated with her grind
I have an eye for excellence
it's the way she moves when she walks
the vibe of her presence
I'm intrigued by her ambition
the sexy of her intuition.

I met Sheba at my first duty station in the Army. She was from Georgia, a true peach. Our connection was instant and we literally spent every moment together. She was a virgin when I met her, and I was cool with it. I don't remember how long she made me wait to experience her physically. I think I don't remember because I was so infatuated with her, so I never felt like I was waiting. I was completely caught up with her. The way I felt about her was just different.

This is more than me
just wanting to be next to you
or a need to have sex with you
I believe in you
I'm invested in you
I know the return reciprocated will be invaluable.

~

She asked me to write for her

but I was lost for words
I was stuck on writers block
between promiscuous ave and monogamous
drive.

She asked me to write for her
must have misinterpreted my directions.

She asked me to write for her
but I tried not to get too deep
'cause I didn't know how she would take it.

She asked me to write for her
so I plagiarized my father's lines
hoping she couldn't read between them.

She asked me to write for her
so I assumed she couldn't process my type
or comprehend my manuscript.

She asked me to write for her
and I was inspired to right my wrongs.

ABOUT A YEAR or so into our relationship, I was about to come up on orders. I wasn't exactly sure where I was going. I knew the time was coming and I wanted her to go with me. The only way it was going to happen though, is if we were married. Kind of makes it sound like I only thought about marrying her because of the Army. While it definitely was a factor, I knew I wanted to be with her. Hell, I was in love!

And you
You're my heart woman

I can feel you before
I'm within your reach
I hear you before
you begin to speak
I can see you when
my eyes are closed
when I'm deep under your water.

I love to breathe and drown in the flow of you
you're the pulse rolling through my beating veins
inject me to keep me from going insane
you're my drug woman
you're good for my health
I must be addicted
'cause for a high of you
I wanna sell to you myself.

I just wanna love you woman
inhale all of you woman
take me to a higher elevation woman
where we can walk around the moon
like stars and create our own constellation
woman.

You light my fire woman
let's melt and pour like hot wax
mold ourselves into mountains
become our higher selves and climax
together we intertwine
like the locks of Samson's hair
means the longer we're together
the stronger our love and I swear
if forever is where you wanna go

then I'm gonna take you there.

God musta put his finger
in the water
when he poured life in you woman
you just too damn fine woman
like that aged fine wine woman
I'd be less of a man
not to acknowledge your presence
even less of man
to ignore such an essence
how could I call myself a man
and not acknowledge these beautiful black
women.

So when I'm down on my knees
I thank God for taking my rib
to expose my heart
to show me how to love
like this woman
strong woman
black woman
understandably misunderstood woman
I would never call you out your name
I just want to show you this love woman.

I remember when I asked her to marry me. It was so childish. I don't remember exactly what I said, but it went something like:

"Hey, I need to tell you something," purposely inserting a tone of guilt accompanied by my best impersonation of a puppy dog.

"Something like what?" she said, her brow dipping a

little in the middle exhibiting a mixed emotion of bewilderment and fiery anxiety.

You know the face your mom makes when you are about to tell her something you did and you know you weren't supposed to do it? The one where you could see in her eyes she's already mentally cocked and loaded for a round of whoop ass? She had the face. I maintained my composure and continued with my "confession."

"Well, I've been doing a lot of thinking about us, and I've been wanting to tell you this for a while, I just haven't been able to bring myself to tell you."

"Tell-me-what?" I could tell she was trying to maintain her cool, but her eyes, I thought I was beginning to see moisture collecting in the wells of her eyes, like morning dew ready to drip off the tip of a leaf. At this point I knew I needed to get on with it.

"Well, I think it's time for us, to move on with our lives," I said inserting a dramatic pause." Will you marry me?"

She didn't respond initially, she just hugged me.

If we gonna come together
then let's become one together
like, let's just stand in the sun and mold together
be forever young by growing old together
let the seasons come and go so we can change together
I mean you can walk your own walk so we can find our path together
drive in different lanes as long as we riding in the same direction together
and we can view the world in different ways to paint the perfect picture together

so when they see you they get a vision of me as
we become one in the same together.

Commitment Vows:
I commit to God, as God has been committed
to me,
I commit to me, so that I can commit to you,
I commit to you, because I am committed to us.

So at nineteen years old I was married, and she was eighteen. Yes, we were young, but it was real. I remember my sister, my third sister, being so upset. She didn't even come to the wedding.

I was a husband before I was a man
Before I ever understood love
Before I knew how to give love
Before I knew how to receive love
Before I knew how to define love
Before I knew how to be love and be LOVED.

I don't think very many people believed in us at first. However, as the years passed it changed. Me and Sheba literally watched each other grow. We had probably been through every sitcom relationship situation you could think of. We were your favorite night time television couple.

"You make me sick,"
as if you're a viral infection
designed to strengthen my immunity
and enhance my protection.
"You get on my last nerve,"
as if you're a pinch

awakening me from a nightmare.
"I can't stand you,"
as if you're a pair of bad knees
keeping me from standing on my own
when I should be kneeling in prayer with you.
"Just leave me alone,"
as if you're an antagonizing fly
just wanting me to acknowledge your presence.
"Kiss my ass,"
as if you're turning me on with your lips
so "Kiss me as" you did the first time.
"Just Shut Up,"
as if life is stressing me out
and silence in your presence is what I need
to keep from shutting down.
"Why'd you do that, say that, act that way,"
as if you know me
and you constantly want to remind me
of when I'm not being
the best version of me.
"I'm tired of you,"
as if your insomnia,
ensures we capture
each moment of us.
"What do you want to eat?"
as if you'll ever decide
between what you have a taste for
and your appetite to just be by my side.
"Whatever,"
as if you're everything that means anything
and when I think I have nothing
you always have something
And it tends to be exactly what I need.

We went through a lot of ups and downs, more ups than downs. My outlook on life began to change. I began to change. By itself it wasn't a negative thing, but I handled it selfishly. Instead of being honest about the changes I was going through, being up front about how I was feeling, I tried to maintain a facade of being the perfect husband.

I was trying to live up to the expectations I assumed existed in the people closest to me. The pressure turned me into someone I was not, or I should say, someone I didn't want to be: my father. As a consequence of my inability to communicate, I started to feel like I was with Sheba out of necessity instead of by choice. It wasn't about that though, it was about me living a lie. Me trying to be something I was not. Some of it was just me lying and being unfaithful... PERIOD.

Once I took a trip to Chicago
I'm not sure why though,
But I did,
and you know how them Midwest winds blow?
Strong, graceful, so free flow
caught me off guard the way that they blow
I was moved by how they lifted me
how cool it felt in my space so,
I was gone with the wind
didn't know how to fly, though.

Once I took a trip to Chicago
I'm not sure why though,
following the steps of my father's shadow
or my alter ego
I don't know,

perhaps that Georgia Sun had become too
sweltering
for this Philly Bro
spread my wings to make shade
who knew I'd catch the breeze of that wind,
though?

I once took a trip to Chicago
I'm not sure why though,
maybe I was looking to get high with her
scale the walls of her Sears Tower
enjoy her skyline
see her waters down by Lakeshore Drive
Browse her best spots on Michigan and State Ave.
cruise her Navy Pier
get my appetite autographed at her Signature
Room on 95th
take a dive into her famous deep dish
until my craving was consumed.

I once took a trip to Chicago
I'm not sure why though,
But I did.
And you know how them Midwest winds blow
strong, graceful, so free flow
caught me off guard
stole my resistance
and so I let go,
took a trip
me, my guilt and my ego
threw caution to the wind
and landed in Chicago.

Would you love me more if I left myself to get
right for you?
Or if I loved myself right, grabbed your soul, and
left with you? I mean would you love me
for me?
Or for the direction I took to get to you?
Like would you rather love the things I do, or the
things I could do for you?
If I sacrificed myself for a better me, or if I sacri-
ficed myself just for you?
I mean like, do I need to sacrifice the way I see
things, so I can see them just like you?
Or sacrifice the way you see me, by toning myself
in a brighter hue?
I mean is loving you expressed by what I'm
willing to give of myself or by what I'm
willing to do for you?

So while we both did some wild shit, ultimately it was me. I don't say it to sound as if I'm being loyal to a code of privacy between us, but I say it because I don't want to distract from the lesson I learned from our marriage.

In truth maybe I gave up. No, I KNOW I gave up. She was willing to take me back and forgive me. Not out of weakness, but because she saw what I couldn't at the time. She understood love in a way I didn't, despite having her right under my nose the whole time. I just couldn't smell the roses. Maybe I was just too focused on discovering what other flowers existed in other gardens. Or maybe the rose bush had become a weed to my vegetable garden and I just needed to grow in my own space.

It broke my heart, to break your heart,
but it was the only way
for me to be wholehearted.

No matter what I say to you
you will hear what you want to hear
No matter how I present myself
you will see me in your mirror as I appear.
No matter how I move
you will place me in your life
where it best fits your needs.
No matter what I think
your train of thought will take you
where your subconscious leads.
No matter how I feel
you can only be in touch
with your own sense of reality.
No matter how I picture my future
your frame of mind will fit the view
from the window of your own mentality.
So the one thing that really matters
is being who I am for me
No matter who it is that you see,
or need,
or want me to be.
Don't take it personal.
Sometimes I need to walk alone
separate myself
to find my way
and get reconnected with myself.

My ego wanted to apologize to her and make it right, to ease my soul. I apologized and chose the hard right by letting her go. I moved on towards karma, no longer afraid to face my wrongs.

I could only truly love her by loving me first.
How could I value an us, without realizing
my own worth?
Love became a tax
I wasn't prepared to afford.
I found myself in debt,
investing love in her without
accounting for self-love.
And suddenly I
felt less of
myself.

Nonetheless, we are good now, and I am grateful for our relationship. I wouldn't say we are best friends, as if we talk everyday or anything. However, we share this unspoken connectedness. She knows I will always have her back and I know she will always have mine. I will say, we share a very unique bond. We always will. I will always hold a special place for her in my heart, as she has been a major factor in who I am today.

I thought I needed you to forgive me to feel
forgiven,
but I found it wasn't until I repented and forgave
myself, I felt the hands of forgiveness massage
my soul.

One thing is for certain, the relationship changed the

way I view marriage. Marriage is no longer a necessity in my life. And it's not about a "fear of commitment!" I was too caught up in what society and religion said a marriage should be, instead of realizing a marriage is whatever I choose to make it.

Spiritually, I think it's important to build a personal relationship with God. As I've built this personal relationship, I've begun to grow emotionally. I am more in tune with what is right, FOR ME, and what is wrong, FOR ME. My sense of morality has grown. The laws of men have become less and less important to me, because my bond with my higher power trumps all of it.

This doesn't lead to chaos in my life because as I've reached higher levels of self-awareness, I've naturally begun to follow a positive path in my environment. I feel more in sync with my surroundings and attract positive things into my life. The laws of men have become almost irrelevant to my day-to-day activities. I don't need them to govern me, because I've begun to self-govern my life in peace.

Now, I'm not saying there is no need for government and laws. Most people never reach the level of spiritual maturity to self-govern. What I am trying to say is, if we are each individuals, each of us will build our own personal relationship with God. And isn't marriage a relationship with God and a relationship with the partner in your life?

Furthermore, if God is Love, then by building our relationship, the love I have for others grows exponentially. I'm not saying I necessarily LIKE everyone! Hell naw, I definitely don't! But now I inherently move in Love and Peace.

Because I understand this, the way I view marriage has changed. If I am an individual who is building a relationship with God and simultaneously building a relationship with another individual who also has a relationship with

God, when we come together in union, this bond, if it's legitimate, by default, extends beyond the laws and traditions of men.

No marriage is stronger than another because of how closely they follow tradition, or the church, or whatever else society tells them is a successful union. A marriage is successful when those in the union decide to focus on their relationships with God and themselves. That's it... that's all.

Sometimes it may require therapy, counseling, etc... But at the root of it all, letting society dictate what my marriage should look like is bullshit. I will not fall into the trap again. If I marry again, it will be because I want to, not because society says I'm supposed to. It won't be out of necessity, not to impress, not to follow tradition, but solely to share in the experience of continuing to build a relationship with God together.

Love is a necessity for marriage, but marriage is not a necessity for love. Just because I am in love with someone doesn't mean the person is the one I should marry. Goals, compatibility, spirituality, etc... All of those things play a role. I could truly be in love with someone who is terrible with finances, economic responsibility, who has past issues to deal with, a temper, or any other red flags we ignore. Should I marry this person if I am in love? Some people would say yes. They would say, "You can learn to grow together, etc..." Hell naw! I'm not going to gamble with my heart AND someone else's based on the assumption they will change.

For me, love is ONLY a piece of the puzzle. There is so much more to be explored. With each new discovery the energy of love will either grow or fade.

Sometimes I watch a sunset and get mesmerized by it. In the moment all I can think is "Damn, does someone else see what I see?" At this point in my life, I can't figure out who I want to see the sunset with. I'm ok watching it by myself. I told myself, when I want to share this moment with someone, they will be who I marry. If she even exists.

She was my dream girl
or maybe the girl of my dreams
the breathe I caught when I was gasping for air
suffocating in this whirlwind
of love affairs
I inhaled her deep
so I could explore
what lies beneath the surface
of her long kiss goodnight
had me dreaming
on cloud 9
or was it really a quarter til midnight?
When the clock strikes 12
will reality transform this fantasy?
Is she my Tinkerbell?
Am I enchanted by her pixie dust?
Am I high, or not high enough?
Am I addicted to her Midas touch?
Holding on to fool's gold?
Am I in a deep sleep,
or deep in love?
Either way,
don't wake me up.

6

KAYLAH

April 13, 2001

I think we should name her Nikaylah. I looked it up and this is what it means:

(Ni) Kaylah - Hebrew meaning is "Like God" or more modern-day meaning is pure. The name Sanaa is a girl's name of Swahili, African origin meaning "work of art; shining light."

My shining light. Our shining light, Sheba and I, that is. Our daughter. Even if God doesn't have any other plans for us, other than to bring her into this world, everything we go through is well worth it.

And You,
You're my feature presentation woman
my flesh, my blood woman

when I look in your eyes I see all that I am
mesmerized by the past that made me a man,
hypnotized by the presence of this fine woman
mystified by the future of being the hand,
the hand that rocks the cradle,
the hand that feeds ya,
the hand that will be your protector,
yet and still the hand that needs ya.
You got my eyes
her smile
their attitude
but you're still your own woman.
Gonna grow to be a strong woman
black woman
understandably misunderstood woman.
You will be called out your name
but always show love woman
and know I love you woman
will always call you my own woman.
And I know the day will come
when extended fingers won't be
the only ones reaching to grasp your hand.
But I'll always hold on
to the fact of knowing my love
can't be out done by any man,
'cause you'll always be part of me woman.
My Achilles Woman
without you I lose the race.
You help me keep my stride
my motivation woman
you give me the want to go on
you give me my drive
funny how such a little woman

can love so enormously
funny how raising you
done flipped the script
and simultaneously indulged
in raising me.
And you're gonna grow to be a strong woman
black woman
understandably misunderstood woman.
You'll be called out your name,
but always show love woman.

That line really says it all. "Funny how raising you done flipped the script and simultaneously indulged in raising me."

Sometimes I write to her, but when I'm finished writing, I can't tell if I wrote to her or to myself.

One thing has always been important to me, to ensure she always recognizes her own worth. I hope she never feels as though she needs a man to validate her.

Work,
but be more than a busy bee.
Change,
but be better than you used to bee.
Have Goals,
Be unique,
not a wanna bee.
Make honey,
but have the sting of a killer bee.
Be humble,
but know you're destined to be
a Queen bee.

You don't need to cover up your flaws for anyone else,
just make-up your mind. You're always beautiful enough.

Don't just think.
Don't just follow your heart.
Think about what makes your heart beat.
Because logic is heartless,
and the heart is illogical.

Get lost in loving yourself,
before you try to find love
in anyone else.

The only time it's the perfect time to give all your love is every time.

Commitment is giving your word and keeping it at the same time.

Dreams about life which are never lived,
become nightmares of regret which never die.

~

Often times your dreams are premonitions
of who you're supposed to be,
not fantasies about someone
you could never be.

~

Own your happiness.
Earn it by believing in and loving yourself
fiercely.
Despite what someone may mean to you, neither
empower them, nor burden them by making
your happiness their responsibility.
Be accountable to you.

~

See Yourself and Be Yourself.
Believe Yourself and Appreciate Yourself.
Examine Yourself and Judge Yourself.
Recreate Yourself and Develop Yourself.
Challenge Yourself and Grow Yourself.
Push Yourself and Balance Yourself.
Expect Yourself and Respect Yourself.
Receive Yourself and Give Yourself.
Know Yourself and Love Yourself.

~

I appreciate the artist you are
the beauty you create
and the pretty you paint,
but it could never makeup for an unsound soul.
Covergirl can cover up the "u,"
but "So-l" still resonates the same.
You can be aesthetically pleasing to
naked eyes who look for reciprocity
with one track minds.
They have no train of thought
or true understanding
of where beauty lies.
Your aesthetics may give a first impression
but your authentic gets imprinted.
Pretty is stimulating,
but organic is refreshing.
A face full of low self esteem
causes you to overlook
how the perfect of your flaws
gives essence to how beautiful
you naturally are,
or could be
if you believed in you more
than who Sephora told you you needed to be,
"Maybelline" more of what you have to say
about you.
Love the bare minerals of your imperfections.
Wear them flawlessly
to conceal this false idea of perfection.
So again,
I truly appreciate the picture perfect image
you can makeup,
just don't let it be the foundation

of what your beauty is made of.

THE HARDEST THING I ever had to do was admit to Kaylah the reasons why Mom and I were separating. I didn't want to hide it, and I don't know if she truly understood everything; she was kind of young at the time. I guess I figured I wanted to get it over with.

It was selfish of me to do it because I wasn't really doing it for the right reasons. I said I needed to tell her because I didn't want to lie to her, but the reality was, I was trying to exonerate myself. I felt guilty and I wanted to rid myself of the guilt as quickly as possible. I wanted to move on. I didn't see it initially, though. It wasn't until we were on a roadtrip from Philly when it all came to a head.

Sheba and I were freshly separated, so we were still attending family functions together, not ready to break the news to everyone. We had taken a trip to Philly to visit family. On the way back, I was talking to Kaylah about something. I don’t quite remember what it was. Whatever it was caused her to snap.

"I hate you! You ruined my life, and you don't understand me! You don't know what I'm going through!" she screamed at me.

I tried to be mad because of her tone, but quickly realized it was the wrong approach to take. I just let her get it out.

Sheba, was sitting in the back seat. I remember her saying, "Get it out baby," almost as if she was egging her on. I didn't address it. I wanted to but, I knew I was wrong. I probably had this coming for a while now. I didn't live with them anymore, so I was sure they had some heart to heart conversations I wasn't aware of: I didn’t need to be, either.

Afterwards, I made sure I put a lot of focus on mending

the relationship I had broken. I knew how my sister had felt about our father. I didn't want that for Kaylah. I promised myself to always be real with her and to listen to her. She taught me to listen. Up until then, I could only hear the sound of my own voice.

7

JEAN GREY

October 19, 2015

I was watching X-men today, and I must say, Jean Grey really resonated with me! In my world though, she is far from fictional. Jean has those telepathic abilities and is one of the most powerful mutants.

Jean is highly empathetic, and has the characteristics of a caregiver and nurturer. The problem with Jean Grey is, she never understands how powerful she is. After she is originally killed, she returns as Phoenix, more powerful than ever.

The Phoenix symbolizes fire. It represents the ability to rise from the ashes: the power of transformation. It also symbolizes the sun. It is recognized as a solar symbol representing rebirth and new beginnings.

The Jean I knew fully embodies these characteristics. I always felt like she had this power over me. The way we grew, fueling one another, giving oxygen to our trauma, our instability, our connection was intense, like fire. I wonder if she will ever find her Phoenix abilities.

We're elements from different lives
walking the straight and narrow
on these parallel lines
which lie on our unconscious minds
designed to keep us perfectly aligned
Can we dare to cross the line?
open our third eye to skew the lie
get on the same plane to get high and recognize
we create change to the things that matter
when we let our elements combine.

We met in college, we were both Math Majors. We were in an Intro to Psychology class together. When I saw her, I thought she was attractive, but honestly, I didn't really pay her much attention.

I had hit a rough patch in my marriage, but I was still married and my only focus was school. The professor had put us in a group project together because coincidentally, we had the same last name. We were both professional about it. As I mentioned, there was no intent. Sometimes our conversations would stray away from school work, but it was still always innocent.

While I was in school, I was always pretty good at math. She was too, but had transitioned from a career in management and needed some polishing of her math skills. She asked me to tutor her, which made sense, as we were already building a comfortable friendship without any of the extra bullshit.

As I'm sure you can imagine, our conversations strayed away from just math or school more consistently and we really got to know each other. One time, I invited her to a cookout at my house. She declined. Sometimes I wonder how different my life would have been if she hadn't declined the invite. Would her actually meeting my wife have kept any growing emotional attachments at bay? I can't say for sure.

Mathematically speaking
me and you
didn't make one
we came together and made two
as I was still me and you were still you
so that's like 1 and 1
or 121
loosely translated, that's 1 to 2
or 1 over 2, 1/2, part of a whole
the paradox being I was whole without you
and you, whole without me
or so we thought
maybe our wholes were designed
to fill a hole in our existence
or a hole in time
whole time, we were ratios
but not proportional
balanced but not equal

just equivalent potentials
what I needed to make me whole
and what you needed to make you whole
were not one in the same
so we can add to one another equitably
but not necessarily equally
I'm not speaking egotistically
I'm thinking beyond measure
mathematically speaking
me and you
don't equal one
we
me and you
created an infinite sum.

Our connection got really intense on many levels. I don't know if I've ever really believed in soulmates, but at the time, I believed if I had one, she had to be it. We really knew each other in a way I had never experienced. I really didn't know how to explain it. We were as mean to one another as we were loving. But not in a toxic way, more in a caring way. We were extremely candid about everything. I don't know if it was good or bad, it just was what it was.

Your soulmate is your personal photographer
a visionary
a Godsend
sent to see that you see you.
They're not fooled by the flash
that is, they're not blinded by the light in you.
They're optics equipped with an infrared
that can see through the dark in you.

They don't see you in the same light as everyone
else
they're on a different spectrum
3rd eye a telescopic lens
seeing you on a deeper level
than you can even see yourself,
identifying where your light dims.
They're not a distraction
but a diffraction
causing your light to bend
changing the latent image of you
by exposing you to you
developing your negatives
so you can be perfectly visible.

Soulmate or not, she wouldn't be my forever. I loved Jean. The problem is, I loved her while I was supposed to be loving Sheba.

I think I denied it for a long time. And up until now I don't even think I've ever said it out loud. But it's my truth.

I met Jean while I was struggling with my demons, and she was struggling with her own, too. We comforted one another at the expense of everyone around us. For her, our relationship was a gift. To me it was a curse.

No matter how good our relationship could have been, I always saw my failed marriage when I looked at her. Of course, this was my own doing. Jean had nothing to do with my choices.

I think it's just what we do sometimes. Even if it's subconsciously. Rather than look ourselves in the mirror and take full accountability, we identify an excuse to rest our responsibilities on. We find some unseen force to lay the blame on... like love. "Love blinded me!" I mean it was the lie

I told myself. Love didn't blind anything, I just couldn't face myself. I guess in a sense it did make me blind.

She spoke to me telepathically
and touched me with her words
She moved me telekinetically
and pulled my world into hers
She used her 3rd eye telescopically
and saw me for who I was
unblurred.
She had this psychedelic love for me
and I was the drug that she preferred.

They say you can't love two people (partners) at the same time. I've always questioned this. Even in the simplest terms, one would then have to question how a mother can love more than one child. The obvious argument is, different types of love for different children. but is it? Is it not just love?

I think confusion comes into play when we try to put love in a box, as if it is one entity or feeling. Is it too hard to fathom love as energy? A current of electricity which travels through resistors and capacitors to reach its source? An energy directed and redirected but never truly turned off, just stored or transferred.

In this aspect of thought, can love then energize more than one light bulb in a circuit? Granted one bulb may shine brighter than the other, as it receives more voltage from the current in a series of circuits, but energy nonetheless can still be supplied to more than one bulb. Even in a parallel circuit, the bulbs could have the same voltage, but not the full potential of current.

What I'm saying is: love has many forms. It is a verb, a

noun and an adjective. From the verb standpoint, I would agree, one can not truly, or fully, love more than one partner. It is impossible to give one light bulb your full energy (voltage and current) if you must supply energy to another. Here neither light bulb can be lit to its full potential.

However, as a noun, one can have love for more than one. This concept is easy enough to comprehend. What I had to learn was I could have love for more than one person, but I could never give either my fullest potential of my energy. Thus, it became important to learn to harness and focus my energy towards one source and not "steal" anyone else's light. The light could be used to illuminate another path, or to light their own path.

Furthermore, I can say “I love you” to more than one human and truly mean it, but it doesn't necessarily mean I'm truly loving them in the way they should be loved. We can look at it as am I loving myself enough and channeling my energy properly? Simply put, I do believe I can love more than one, but I don’t think I could ever give more than one human the love and full potential of the energy they truly deserve.

Over time Jean became my safe place. For a long time I thought she would be the one I’d marry. I kept waiting to want to share sunsets with her, but whenever I watched the sunset, her image never materialized in my mind. So I just kept looking. Jean and I were in an on and off again relationship for years. There was always something missing though, and I could never quite put my finger on what it was. I still thought she would be my one, but remember I told you, she had demons as well.

You were too picture perfect
so in my broken frame of mind

I kept looking for a blemish in you,
and I found it.
Then fell in love with this perfectly flawed image
of you
tainted in just the right hue
precisely out of focus
exposing the best of you
at just the right angle
where both your ambient light
and dark shadows
create the highest resolution of you.
Just know that when I tell you you're beautiful
it's because I appreciate
each and every unfiltered pixel of you.

She was my definition of beauty
before I knew how to pronounce her name
what I smiled about
before I could express ideas
I must've been born with her on my mind
so I knew her when I saw her
but I was lost for words
she walked right out of my imagination
a dream that I wanted to hibernate in
the scent of her had me high
opened my 3rd eye and I refused to blink
afraid to lose sight of her in the clouds
somewhere.
I didn't know how to pronounce her name.
so I called her
"Beautiful."

"Beautiful" to her was the prelude to pain.

"Beautiful" to her was a war cry.
"Beautiful" was the sweet nothing he whispered
in her ear
before he took everything from her.
"Beautiful" kissed her in her dreams and gave her
nightmares.
"Beautiful" was her scar.
"Beautiful" stole her heart before I ever uttered the
words.

To me she was beautiful
to her, so was I.

I respect her too much to get into the details of her personal demons, though I do believe they played a role in the faltering of our relationship. I began to realize the reason I couldn't see her when I looked at the sunset was because she hadn't grown over the course of our relationship. No, not true. She just hadn't grown with me. There were things she was dealing with, or maybe hadn't dealt with, which kept her from being the woman I knew she could be.

For all the flaws she saw,
I only saw a collage of God's fingerprints.

***

Whenever we get in rhythm you bring the blues..

You see the entire time I was on a personal journey. I was discovering so many things about myself. I guess I expected the same for her. However, it wasn't her story. It wasn't where she was on her life's journey. She felt she already knew what she wanted. She just wanted me. That's all, and her kids of course. Her kids trumped all, and rightfully so. I got to watch them grow up. I was very careful never to play the role of the father in their lives. Perhaps a part of me knew their mother and I weren't forever. They were, and are, great kids. I miss them sometimes. She aspired to be a wife and a mom, and that was it. Maybe a part of me thought less of her because of it. I thought she should want more. I wanted her to match my energy. It was unfair of me. I didn't see it at the time, though.

I don't want to be your one
I'd rather take this second to
allow you
to just be in your own space
I'm not a regret
so let the high come down
and choose me sober
with conscious thought
your first after thought
after you thought about us without
undermining your own selfish thoughts
think it over
Get exhausted loving yourself first
then let me be your second wind.

What I saw was someone who was lost and just choosing complacency over truly finding herself. I remember the day I decided I needed to separate myself from her. We were sitting in the car just talking and I asked her a question. "What are your goals?" She really didn't have a clear answer. Any answer she gave involved her kids or me. It was the moment I realized I wasn't good for her. She saw a fantasy in me, and didn't see the reality in herself. Her fantasy was based on my reality, and to me, it wasn't good. I didn't want to be responsible for her happiness. What did she want for HER?

The question took us down a rabbit hole. Not the one leading to a wonderland, either. All this time had passed and we weren't growing together. So I left. Well kind of left. We still maintained a solid friendship, we were really good friends, and really good lovers, if nothing else.

She reminded me of who I was supposed to be
and I reminded her of her fantasy
in this twisted reality
where I was at battle with myself
war of the rose-bush
became a thorn in my side
battle scared
I was afraid her touch would hurt
or afraid my loyalty to monogamy was cursed
I could only break this spell
by loving myself first.

I didn't push you away to see you fall
I was pushing you over the hump
I wanted to push you to fly
when you were afraid to jump
but pushing you
to push yourself
was pushing me away
from what I wanted.

I realized what I was holding on to

was weighing me down
so I had to let go
to free my hand
so I could reach
for higher ground
and I gained a better perspective
of my downfalls
from the view
I have now.

We tried maintaining a friendship, for some time after that. We had sex sometimes too, but the simple truth was, I had moved on. I could tell she was still in love with me, and maybe I still loved her too, but for me, love wasn't enough. She had things she needed to deal with and I could no longer allow my presence to be her therapy. I wanted her whole, but I never got to know her whole person. I would only know Jean, but I would never witness her transformation to Phoenix. Instead I would be her fire, just as she was mine.

Don't love me because it's comfortable,
but because when it gets uncomfortable
loving me is still easy.
Don't love me to avoid being alone,
but because when you're alone
you can't avoid loving me.
Don't love me because you don't want to endure
the process
of finding love in someone else,
but because loving me is a part of the process
in you loving yourself.
Simply speaking, don't settle for me,

but if through all of life's unsettling complexities
you still feel settled by me,
then please,
confidently love me.

SHE WANTED to believe I had moved on because of another woman. I let her believe it, but I knew otherwise. I did indeed fall in love, but I had fallen deeply in love with myself. I knew I wouldn't have gotten to this point if not for our relationship. I grew so much over the period of time we were together and I desperately wished she had, too. Perhaps she did, but as I mentioned, it just wasn't with me.

I thought I needed to be in love with her to love myself
but I could only love her enough to let her go
and forgive myself enough
to keep hold of the lesson to let myself grow.
I had to let her hate me today
so she could wake up from the dream
and still love herself tomorrow.
I fed her my truth
ate my own words
and lost my breath trying to swallow.
I choked on my pride
and let my ego die
so she could be free
living a life un-captivated
by the idea of us
living a lie.

~

Did I let go,
or did you not keep up?
Did you feel the growth and change in me
or do you feel I gave up?
Did I lie
or did I wake up?
Did I do something to you
or did you do nothing for yourself?

~

I don't just think.
I don't just follow my heart.
I think about what makes my heart beat,
as my logic can be heartless,
and my heart so illogical.

~

Hey...
never forget how beautiful you are,
how great you are,
and what you have to offer the world.
Always take time to meditate
and show gratitude to the Universe
... have a good day.

Our relationship didn't end abruptly, it dissipated over time, which was a direct reflection of how we had met. Our conversations began to change. She would always tell me about how well she was doing, and I was happy for her. It seemed as if she was finally finding herself.

The problem was I couldn't tell if she was genuine or if there was a hidden agenda behind telling me about all the positivity transpiring in her life. Either way, I was happy for her, but in the back of my mind, I was like "why now? Why are you becoming this... Phoenix of Jean now?" She seemed to be such a better person without me. I know she is, and her story is not mine to tell. I could only respect her transformation. Similarly, the man who left the relationship was not the same man who entered it. Without the experience of her, I don't know who I'd be right now.

I hope you don't think you
suddenly wanting to be a better you
AFTER me
would breed envy in me
or even be insulting to me
it's just confirmation to me
we weren't meant to be.
You were only willing to be
a fraction of you for me
so how could you have been the one for me?

Reflecting.
Was I there?
Did I live to love like
you did? Was I as scared
as you were when light became dark?
It wasn't beautiful. Was it initially?

Initially it was beautiful, wasn't it?
Dark became light. When? Were you as
scared as I was? Did you
like, love to live? I did.
There I was,
Reflecting.

8

TOO MUCH OF HER

November 29, 2015

What's so wrong with being single? One of my co-workers told me, I need to grow up, I'm immature. Why? because I'm not ready to, or have no intentions of, being in a monogamous relationship. Why is it not ok to explore? I don't think there is anything immature about it. I do think, however, in living this lifestyle, it's important to understand my journey to find a mate is no different than one of someone who seeks monogamy.

Being single doesn't mean I get to pick from a buffet line. It means I should be ordering from a different menu all together. I really shouldn't be entertaining relationships with people who are looking to build something lasting. I still have the responsibility of protecting the essence of women. In my opinion, women are more emotionally expressive than men. This is not to say women are more emotional. Those are two different sentiments, and I don't believe the latter to be true. However, the former, at least within the bubble of my experience, seems to be accurate.

The main difference I find is women transition quicker than men do in the decision making process of choosing to be in a committed relationship. I'm not interested in engaging in the gender or sex wars currently permeating social media, but I just believe men and women think differently, generally speaking.

Either way, as a single man, I bear the obligation of engaging with companions who agree with and are in the same position in life I am. There are plenty of women who are at places in their life where they don't want anything serious at the time or just want a fling, etc... Plenty for me to choose from.

It is also important to understand single relationships require the same level of communication and accountability as committed relationships, or maybe even more because feelings change quickly. Whatever standards or rules one holds for the relationship they wish to be in needs to be communicated and reciprocated consistently.

The likelihood of undesirable emotional outcomes in these types of relationships is high, the potential for long term friendship is low, and finding true satisfaction is moderate at best.

Wanting to be single does not excuse me from the responsibilities of being in a relationship, because regardless of what the endgame is, it's still a relationship which requires communication and honesty. The lifestyle I choose to live, doesn't necessarily imply maturity. Hell, I could argue immaturity for choosing complacency or conformity, instead of going through the gauntlet of finding true love.

Crazy how I can articulate this so well, but still find myself making waves where others are wading. Those waves have rippling effects, ultimately, I'm drowning myself.

I had to change my cards and stop playing hearts
quit cutting the deck and play a better hand.
I pulled the Queen of Spades
put on my poker face
maybe she would be the one to get me straight
flush out my true intentions
I couldn't play a full house
despite how I was raised
she tried to call my bluff

all my cards on the table
and she realized the high pair she saw
wouldn't be enough.

Be careful, my savage looks like Prince charming and feels like an orgasm, sounds poetic, but can leave you damaged. I'll apologize now, for sexing you so unapologetically, and loving you so pathetically. I tend to be reckless, drunk driving your body wild, so don't be fooled by my smile. My hard truth hurts so good, it's both pleasure and pain. I use my tongue intelligently so both the spread of your legs and your sapiosexuality fall in love with my brain. We can enjoy this moment in ecstasy and create a beautiful memory. Just don't fall in love with me.

At some point I came to the realization marriage or monogamy just wasn't for me. Despite everything I had learned from my previous relationships and despite what I thought I knew about love and about myself, I hadn't begun to scratch the surface.

I was living the life: in my mid thirties, no young children (my daughter was a young adult,) financially stable, and no attachments. I loved living this life. I considered myself to be a conscientious brother, and I was, on the surface.

My problem was I was making waves in water where

others were wading. I was always very upfront about my intentions, but when I realized they wanted more, I would let it linger on until something happened, ie: they got tired of the shenanigans and moved on.

I was very intentional in everything I said, but my actions weren't lining up. What I didn't realize was I was treating women I had no intention of building anything substantial with, as if I did want something more. I've always been emotionally intelligent, and a good conversationalist, plus I always treated women with respect and was a gentleman. Not to say there was anything wrong with these attributes, generally speaking.

I am a sapiosexual who tends to get aroused when
the curve of her mental figure knows how to
calculate the perspective which catches my
third eye, and gets me to speak my mind. She
can be so moved by the accent of intelligence
in my street smart dialect, she falls into the
hypnotic spell of my brain waves and it
makes her wet, her sapiosexual also turned on
by the size of my intellect, and we then lie in
the naked truth of understanding by having a
one night stand of amazing brain sex.

However, I was applying them in a way to give off a false sense of reality. I was giving more of myself than I should have. By doing that, my actions were saying "I'm willing to be more than casual." In my mind, I was just being me. I genuinely liked and cared for these women.

I didn't love them though. I made some very genuine connections, but at the end of the day, I just didn't want anything more than casual friendship. I didn't know how to regulate it. I thought I was communicating it properly, but communication extends beyond words. This wasn't always the case, as sometimes there was definitely some misrepresentation happening by some women who thought they could "change" me. Either way, I was never truly happy at the end of the day. Maybe it's because subconsciously I really did want to be in a meaningful relationship, but I was too caught up in the high of ascertaining temporary gratification without accountability.

You can like me or lust me,
just don't love me, like,
maybe you can love me horizontally,
but just don't go 90 degrees on me
and try to take this high vertically.

They say actions speak louder than words,
but the good you feel from the touch of me
doesn't speak the truth of the savage in me
listen to my war cry
follow my tear drops to where they lie
- next to me,
but they're like acid rain,
so not too close.

I'm into you, but not inside of me.
I'm a sinner, but not a liar,
so want me objectively,
less I leave you with a lot to be desired.
I am not exonerated by the honesty in my voice,
but I offer you these words of choice.

I can give you the most of me,
just not the best part of me,
see I'm still looking for the piece of the puzzle,
it's lost somewhere in me.

9

KARMA

May 5th, 2018

The last thing she said to me was, "Karma is a bitch!", as if I just completely did her dirty. I hate when people do that. How they tend to interpret one negative action as an indicator of a person's whole being. It's like they completely disregard someone's positive characteristics if something they don't like is done. The hypocrisy is, those same people expect empathy when they make bad decisions, wanting others to weigh their good behavior when being judged for their wrongs.

It's all good, I don't even think that's how Karma operates. "Karma's a bitch?"

I don't think so, but I had to look that shit up to make sure! And just as I thought,

Karma is defined as the effect stimulated by

the summation of a person's actions in their current and previous state of being. Therefore, Karma is neither good or bad, she is a mediator between who we are and our higher selves. She is a woman of action who isn't afraid to do what needs to be done to guide us to where we need to be in life. Karma inspires growth, change, responsibility, focus, connection, patience, and peace of mind. Karma is a reflection of self, forcing us to examine our past selves.

So, they may say Karma is a bitch, but I personally think she's simply misunderstood. I realized this once I took the time to get to know her... Once I took the time to get to know me.

I met Karma at a house gathering and we hit it off pretty quickly. We had really good sexual chemistry and we were really cool as well. Neither one of us was looking for anything serious, but we had fun together. She was still dating and so was I. In fact, we would often discuss our dates with one another. We didn't hide anything from one another, as there wasn't a reason to. The thing I liked most about Karma is she matched my energy. She gave whatever I was giving. She would never really say anything, it was always in her actions. It made it easy to be around her because I always knew what to expect. However, it all changed when she found out she was pregnant.

She asked me if I loved her and I was empathetic,
yet lacked reciprocity, I mean.

I loved the way she loved me
perhaps because I didn't love myself enough
or maybe I loved myself too much,
selfishly instead of selflessly.
There were things I loved about her
but truth was,
I knew I could live life without her.
Yet I continued to rent space in her temple
within her walls
disturbing her peace and invading her privacy,
but she had invited me.
When I stood outside her threshold knocking
perhaps she thought I was opportunity
waiting to give her true love finally.
She failed to recognize the vampire who resided
inside of me
waiting on her blessing to come inside and suck
her dry
both literally and figuratively
but I mean, I never lied to her,
not with these lips
except maybe when they kissed her
perhaps my energy stunned her
ran down her spine causing her to lose her grip
pried her hands off her pride and resistance
and her resistance off her essence and so she
let go,
but no, I never lied to her.
She asked me if I loved her, so I told her,
"I don't think I can love you in the way that even
I understand,
nor in the way that really makes sense,
but I want to learn your language,

so I know exactly how to speak to you in your
feminine dialect,
and let my masculine accent vibrate with your
Chi and make you wet",
I guess I could have just said I wanted to talk
dirty and have sex,
but I was feeling poetic,
so I spoke to her poetically,
making it her responsibility
to decipher my metaphor for what it really was,
though retrospectively I was subconsciously
attempting to be verbally pleasing to her sapio-
sexuality
while using the attraction of our physical beings
to separate her legs and logic from her reasoning.
I used the manipulation of my tongue,
but I never lied to her,
I only lied WITH her, physically,
and spiritually when I tried to conceptualize
my nonsense as innocence,
and her too when she told herself,
"If I love him enough, I can love him into
loving me,"
as if this infatuation was more than just sex.
She was wet behind the ears in love,
slowly drowning in this gravitational pool of lust
mistaking my back stroke for a touch of affection
my breast stroke for a heart connection
to her this temptation felt like a vibe
to me she was a flute of fine wine
and I was binge drinking her
getting drunk off her
pouring myself into her

not realizing I was filling her up with regret
until her cup runneth over, my cold shoulder
into my lukewarm soul.
I felt the need to console her,
hold her, reconnect kinetically
transferring energy
magnetically attracting her misconception to my deception,
and her womb to the flow of my seed.
She had become the bearer of my fruit
unknowingly she had picked from a rotten tree.
Our roots didn't run deep & they weren't intertwined,
I didn't nurture her nature,
and so the legacy of me fell
like a dead leaf onto infertile soil,
and I can't help but wonder, If it's because I lied with her
that my legacy died with her,
but I never lied to her,
not as much I was lying to myself,
admittedly I never loved her,
I only loved myself,
or I should say I only loved me,
as my self was starved of the God in me,
while I was feeding the savage in me,
until I was constipated internally,
full of my own shit,
I had to go 10 toes down,
man up so I could see over the mound of it,
to realize God is in self,
and God is love,
and Self love was a necessity to give love,

and giving love was a necessity to being loved,
and truth was I just wanted to Be Loved,
and just Be LOVE...
She asked me if I loved her...
and I apologized to her,
and told her,
I'm still learning to love myself,
I can only give you my truth,
and let you decide where you want to lie,
but I won't lie to you, to lie with you,
and I won't lie with you if I'm not aligned
with you,
I want to vibe with you,
She asked me if I loved her,
and I told her,
No.

When she told me she was pregnant, I was floored. I remember trying to reflect on every sexual encounter, tried to relive every moment to prove to myself it couldn't be real. Perhaps it was someone else's. We had discussions about children and both agreed we didn't want any, at least not now. Or maybe I told her I didn't want any and she just agreed with me to avoid the conversation.

I remember asking her what she wanted to do. She returned my question with a question. I felt like she already knew what my response would be and she just wanted to validate it. I told her I didn't want to have children, but I would go along with whatever she wanted to do. The latter of the statement I said only because I didn't want to be a total dick. However, my demeanor had already spoken for me.

There was more than one reason I didn't want to have a

child. You see, I had met someone else, and Karma knew it. She knew I had recently met someone I was really into. I didn't hide it from her. When I told her, she initially played it cool, but I could tell it was bothering her, as something had changed between us. The exhilarating feeling we once felt from the free fall of our relationship had come to the end on the line, and we were now just holding on to the bungee cord, going through the ups and downs, waiting for it to all end.

I told her I had met ***Miami***, that's what I called her, and explained I really liked her. However, Miami and I were far from being in a committed relationship, so I didn't see any reason to stop talking to Karma. As I mentioned, we were really good friends.

When I shared this with Karma, I think she started reevaluating her choices and what we were doing. I think the idea I could possibly choose to be with someone else after everything we shared bothered her. I couldn't blame her for it either, because there wasn't anything "wrong" with her or our relationship. It was just Miami made me feel ... different. At the time, I didn't know how to explain it.

Eventually Karma decided she wanted to keep the baby. Her reasons weren't about me. Karma was a very spiritual individual. She was heavy into meditation practices, crystals, and things of that nature. It was one of the things I liked about her. To her, the pregnancy had a deeper meaning in connection with her family, generational curses, and just growth and change within herself. Physically, she wasn't even sure she could even get pregnant. I couldn't be mad at her decision, I respected it. It didn't change the fact I really didn't want to have a child, though. I accepted what was to come and tried to prepare myself mentally.

A few weeks passed of me trying to wrap my head

around what was about to happen. Our relationship wasn't the same anymore. It was difficult for me to act like I was happy about something I wasn't, and she knew it. Remember when I told you she always gave what I was giving? She called me, "Can you come over?" she asked.

"Yeah, is everything ok?" I responded inquisitively.

"Yeah, I just want to talk."

When I got to her apartment, I knew something was up because her father was there and the energy was off. We went into her bedroom and she told me she had a miscarriage and she was going to have surgery. That's why her father was in town. The surgery was to be the next day. I stayed the night with her and then met her and her father at the hospital the next day. Everything felt really awkward. We would never be the same after this and I knew it.

While in the waiting room her father and I had a conversation. He was a very cool dude, I really liked him. He said to me, " You know she is smitten with you. She doesn't want to admit it, but she is. She never told me it, but I know my daughter and the way she talks about you, the way she acts around you, the way her demeanor changes when you're around. That's why this is so hard for her."

It was a hard pill to swallow. I think I already knew it, but hearing it out loud from her father hit hard. He could have very easily been cussing me out, ready to beat my head in, but he saw the truth of the matter and he wanted me to hold myself accountable for what had happened in all this. He didn't outright say it, but I was able to read between the lines. Suddenly her losing the baby really hurt. I had come to the realization the miscarriage was partially my fault. Karma needed my positive energy, not the negativity of my selfishness.

A few days later I was at Karma's house and she asked

me about Miami. I told her I had told Miami about everything and she didn't want anything to do with me.

"How do you feel about that? Are you still going to try to be with her?" I could hear the vexation in her voice, and I could feel her energy shift.

"Yeah, I'm going to try," I said.

"Well, I guess this just all worked out for you, huh?" she said sarcastically. Her stare burned into me and she didn't blink at all. Her face was blank. She was examining my reaction to her statement.

I knew she was talking about the miscarriage. The truth was, she was right. However, I never wished it at all. I had already come to terms with the fact she was having our baby.

"Why would you say some shit like that!" I said. I was quite annoyed by her statement. Somewhat because there was some truth to it, but mostly because I felt like it was an attack on my character. I didn't want it for her, not in the least, but damn I could understand why she would say what she said.

In the moment, I knew it could never be the same for us. I knew she blamed me for her miscarriage and I knew the situation had built up to a level of resentment I wouldn't be able to overcome.

I felt horrible, the level of guilt and regret I felt was unreal. The pain I was feeling was beyond just guilt. Everything came flooding in as I started reflecting on all of my relationships and how I treated these women. How I was treating myself. I started wondering about the baby who was no more. I felt lost.

Ironically, I had actually just found myself and didn't realize it. Karma had forced me to look at the summation of myself. The good and the bad. I was able to see myself and become fully aware of what I needed to work on to grow and change. She had unlocked past truths and traumas I had locked away, bringing everything full circle.

This relationship placed a
strain on her,

tears couldn't
restore what had been depleted,

she poured,
until she was empty.

10

TROUBLE

She was so good at being bad,
and I was so bad at being good,
I guess opposites attract,
she became good company,
when I was doing bad all by myself.

I met her at an after party. When I saw her I instantly knew I had to talk to her. I was confident in my approach with her, but not in an arrogant way. There was this assurance I had, like something was telling me I was supposed to know her. "Do you see her right there?" I said tapping my frat brother on his shoulder and pointing.

"Yeah, she's tough! Sheesh!" he said squinting to get a better look.

"I'm a get her number." He chuckled as if to say, "whatever" when I said it. "Watch me," I said assertively.

Truth was, I had no idea what I was going to say. My talk was simply to build myself up. I was never afraid to talk to a woman I was interested in. It was never really my style. I normally just laid low and waited for the right opportunity.

Like a lion stalks a gazelle, only difference was, I didn't hunt the weakest of the herd, I preferred the challenge of going after the most regal of them. Just as I was thinking it, I made eye contact with her.

The feeling I felt from her eye contact had
me high
the sight of her was so damn stimulating to me
had my masculinity wanting to feel the finesse
of her feminine caress
something about a woman's touch captivates
the beast in me
gets me locked in.
Her presence was an aphrodisiac
I was yearning to unwrap
and get to know more intimately,
so I could show my appreciation for
God's gift.
I saw that she saw me see her
and that uplifted me,
cut into me,
exposing my intentions
my stare was binge drinking her
until my mind was drunk driving my body wild
but she didn't blink,
I guess she too, was feeling untamed,
like a lioness she was devouring my attention,
so I spoke
she heard me growl
and when I growled
it made her purr
our animal instincts had kicked in and we
were both

stalking sin
our attraction had threw our inhibitions
into this Lion's Den.
I took my shot
and got drunk from her nectar.
I was hung over
operating under her influence
driving myself crazy trying to get sober
walking the thin line between love and lust
head spinning,
trying to maintain my composure.

Once I spoke to her, my intuition was confirmed. "Hey, why you look so mad, you should smile," I said. She gave me a half smile. Damn, she was even prettier than I initially thought.

She makes me smile
not like curving
the corners of my lips
teeth clenched,
'cause she's amusing to me,
but because she jolts
a wave of inspiration in me
she's a muse to me,
a move in me,
she's moving me
it's her presence,
gifting me,
her vibe vibrant
indicative of my inner chi
stimulating this energy in me.
She operates on a high frequency

her connection sends
this shockwave through me
her internal and external beauty
like two tips of a taser
electrifying to me
turning on this light in me
I'm tapped in.
She's wired differently
a conduit to source energy
like Miriam Exodus 15
amplifying the God in me
her smile makes me smile.

She didn't say much initially, and neither did I, but sometimes it's what isn't said which says everything. She was difficult to read, but I was still intrigued by her. People often say it about me as well, so coming from her, it didn't turn me off. We conversed off and on throughout the night, and each conversation opened up a little more.

She was a hardcover
written in fine print
literally a literary work of art
whose literature wasn't for the illiterate
or spiritually illegitimate
or those lacking emotional literacy.
You see, inquiring what was inside of her
required you to decipher her
not decide for her
as her train of thought
didn't "trains-late"
for a one track mind,
but I was prompt

and re-read her lines a few times
as I was dying to get to know her.
I buried myself in her
studied her
to interpret her
researched her
to learn her ropes
and wrapped my mind around
her syntax, well written,
eloquent and complex,
but see, I was a cognitive reader
so to me she was a good read
and I understood her phonetically
comprehensively
read her prolonged prologue intimately.
I got to know her
prior to pouring over
the main body
blank pages waiting
to be written
an unabridged
story of us.

April 8, 2016

Last night I drove Christa home. It was all innocent though, I had no intentions of trying to sleep with her. I mean, if she woulda tried, I don't think I woulda turned her down. But honestly, it wasn't even dat kind of vibe. And to be completely honest, I was actually glad we didn't have sex or anything. Don't get me wrong, there was definitely sexual chemistry. It was just, something about her felt...different. I ain't decide if it's a good or bad thing yet. However, I do know if we woulda smashed last night I wouldn't be writing this, so there's that. In any case, we had some good convo, it was intimate AF, and I really enjoyed it. I got her number so yeah, I'm a see what she about.

I saw her beauty
but when she spoke I saw her crown
I saw her sexy
but when she moved I saw the royalty in
her gown
I saw the full of her lips
but when she smiled I saw her positive vibe
I saw her Egyptian eyes
but when she stared
I saw the consciousness of her mind
I saw the smooth of her skin
but when she exhaled I saw the diamond
from the rough she'd been in
I saw the soft of her curves
but when she stood the straight of her back
showed the strength of her character within
I saw the soft of her hair
but when she touched me
I saw the vitality of her soul
I saw her feminine

but when she showed me who she was
I saw a Queen to behold.

Her curves can turn my eye,
but it's the contour of her intellect
that turns my mind
the trajectory of her conversation
that turns my time
into an investment well spent.
I'm intrigued by how she exposes
the simple mindedness of complexities
it's mind bending.
I can see her curves
but it's her way with words
it's the way she walks without moving
the earth seems to move under her feet
like she's on a treadmill
making the world turn,
pulling me into her
attracting my sapiosexuality
you see it's not her figure for me
it's how she figures
and her ability to stimulate
the intricacies of me so intimately.

It's not the Physical Beauty
It's the Intellectually Sexy
the Spiritually Pretty
the Emotional Maturity
for me.

YOU MAY BE WONDERING why I called her Trouble. We were having a conversation once and she was telling me about how she really wasn't looking for a relationship. She just wanted to have fun, but dudes always ended up liking her more than she liked them. She didn't hide the fact she was playing the field, and I respected it. Shit, so was I. Problem was I knew I already liked her, so I called her Trouble, a reminder to myself to not fall for her.

She wasn't a whore
she just enjoyed
exploring herself more
than losing herself
within the perspectives
of misogynistic views.
She was at a point in her life
where being tailored
to a relationship
didn't suit her well.
It was too restrictive
to her free mind
too tight around
her waistline.
It was trying to squeeze her hips
to get her to fit
into society's chastity belt
while her male counterparts
were encouraged
to live life loosely.
She had experienced
all the bumps in the road
from the potholes as a backseat passenger
on joy-rides
as male pride had shotgun
with the intent to blow her back out

and love her from behind.
She has since found her own drive
intent on getting exhausted loving herself first
ride her second wind.
That's the silver lining of it all
she now recognized herself as the grand prize
covered in gold dust to enhance her shine
but don't be confused,
she didn't bare her minerals
to play the rigmarole
of a Jezebel looking for good time.
She understood how to refrain from an
overdose of pheromones and dopamine
to maintain a clear mind.
She compartmentalized compliments
and ruled her beauty
with her own eye.
She was a matriarch
taste testing fine wine.
She was selective,
not to be selected or picked
out of a line up by male egos
as if being a woman was a crime.
she loved herself fiercely,
and would choose her King wisely.
To her there was more at stake
than the burn she felt
from the eyes of those conformed
to this Salem society.
She had nothing to be ashamed of
and everything to be proud of
she didn't decide to irresponsibly spread her legs
she had simply decided

to be responsible for opening her own mind
not to spread herself thin,
but to lay her independence on thick
which was a hard reality
for some to swallow.
She actually owned her body.
She wasn't beyond monogamy,
she just unapologetically learned
to love simultaneously
embracing her mind,
body and soul
all at the same time.
She would only love a man who loved her
and himself within the same context.
She wore her fuck 'em dress
to celebrate her celibacy to giving a fuck
to what anyone else thought of her
because the way ***SHE*** *loved*
her - self - love
was the most amazing sex.

I was ok with the fact she was exploring herself. I didn't judge her or ask questions either. It would have been hypocritical of me, as I was still on my own journey of self-discovery. I liked her and was really enjoying getting to know her. I wanted her. The Universe had other plans for ~~me~~ *us* though, and as ***Karma*** would have it, I learned she was moving to ***Miami*** in a few months. I figured I had just met her at the wrong time in my life.

I found myself in trouble
knee deep in hot water
but when I wiped away the steam,

I saw myself clearer.

I didn't go looking for trouble,
but trouble found me
hiding in the backwoods
high off life.
I inhaled,
smelled trouble
I knew trouble was brewing
she was bitter-sweet.

Maybe I caused trouble,
but trouble-make-her sexy to me,
attracted me
I knew she would be worth the trouble.

11

MIAMI

I found ***Trouble*** in ***Miami.*** Good trouble of course.

March 8, 2017

My first trip to Miami, and I found out exactly what Miami was all about! The vibe in Miami was CRAZY! It's like a city high on caffeine all the damn time...the energy, culture, festivities, art, the nightlife... hell yeah, I had a good damn time. One thing I definitely learned about Miami is despite how stylish and elegant she may seem, Miami still harbors a ghetto charm. Perhaps not charming to someone who can't relate, but being from Philly, there's nothing more soothing than the nostalgia of being in the essence of what feels familiar.

She was an artist,
and I was a work of art in progress.
She was drawing me into her space
like a painting within the edges of her canvas.
She wanted to cover the pencil sketched smudges
left by the previous mistakes she tried to erase,
but if you blew the residue of graphite you
could see the fingerprints left by those who
made her heart break,
but I was oil based,
and she didn't see me in black and white.
She saw vibrant,
making her canvas vibrate
until it was blank slate
and so we vibed and conversed
about the art we would create.

I liked Miami and I would visit her often. Outside of our visits, we would communicate using this app called Marco Polo. It allowed us to talk to one another around our busy schedules. Basically you could record a facetime and then the receiver could watch it later. I'm not an iphone user, so it was a good alternative.

We really got to know each other because we were both really open and free. We didn't have any titles, so our only expectations of one another were the ones we discussed intimately. I knew her boundaries and she knew mine. When things changed, for either of us, we were open about it. I've never been in an open relationship, but what we had was probably pretty close to it. It was different because we were long distance. I think we were mature and real about our situation. Well, at least that's how we put on.

Her vibe converted
the things I only knew potentially
into something more kinetically.
She had put emotions into motion,
her field of energy
attracted my inner chi
and I was drawn to her
so magnetically
as I pictured us in a bond
not merely physical
but on a higher level mentally
to enhance the state of our being,
magnify her naked truth.
I wanted to believe what I was seeing.
I saw where her beauty lies
and was more enticed by her flaws,
admired her desire to grow spiritually
so I knew eventually they'd fall off.
The Universe had so intentionally
positioned her
where my third eye could see
to inspire me
to be closer to the God in me
to be strong enough
to handle the intensity
of simply holding her hand.

ONE OF THE things I enjoyed most about Miami was her independence. She didn't need me. As a man, it may sound kind of weird, but I didn't want to be with someone who needed me for anything. I felt as though if they needed me, our connection would be based on me supplying the need. Alternatively, if I was with someone who solely wanted me, everything else would fall into place.

This is not to say I wanted someone who didn't expect anything from me, nor someone who wouldn't hold me to a certain standard. It's not what I'm referring to. Do I expect to provide in a relationship? Absolutely. However, do I want to be with someone who doesn't have ambitions of their own and relies on me to provide them with everything? Probably not. Unless of course they plan on being a housewife. Thing is, I have never really been attracted to the housewife type of woman. I'm attracted to ambition.

I don't think any less of a woman who wants to be a housewife and rely solely on a man for her livelihood. For me, I like being with someone who matches my energy, or at least is secure enough within themselves to understand me.

Do I expect to be held accountable for the way I treat the woman in my life? I do, but ultimately, I am not responsible for someone else's happiness. I am not responsible for how they love themselves. If they cannot find happiness or love within themselves, then how can they truly love me? Miami matched my energy.

Who knew me striking up a conversation with
you would ignite a spark in our first contact
to make us the perfect match,

creating this fire we make, love won't extinguish
as it's been gaslit by a flint of lust until we
saw our feelings catch,

then we fanned the flames kindling embers which
glowed and attracted,

this ***fume*** *that we turned into* ***fusion***
by taking the focus off ***~~u & me~~*** *and putting an* ***i***
on us,

maybe it's the controlled burn we set
that stimulated new growth in us,

until we spontaneously combust
and return to star dust.

Just because it seems like I'm putting myself
before you,
doesn't mean I don't adore you
it means I want more for you
you see, me putting everything into me isn't me
living selfishly
it's me wanting to give you the best of me
selflessly
learn to walk with me silently
don't speak with insecurities
and you'll hear you and me simultaneously.

I don't want you to need me
I need you to want me
I don't want you to need me to breathe
I just need you to want to breathe me

inhale me freely
'cause I don't want to suffocate you
I just want to fill you
and make you feel so good on the inside
so you refuse to exhale me
so you choose to hold your breath.

I REMEMBER when I told her Karma was pregnant. Everything changed. I didn't know how I expected her to react, but I knew I wasn't going to lie to her about it. It didn't even cross my mind. When I found out about the pregnancy, it was the middle of the work day. I reached out to Miami right away. I was at work, so I left her a Marco Polo message. She never called me back.

In the evening, I was at home pondering life. I had just finished my daily meditation ritual and with nothing pressing to occupy my time, I just sat in my thoughts. The room was barely lit, moonlight sparingly entering through the edges of the blackout drapes. The sound of running water from the fish tank was tranquil, enhanced by my favorite Neo Soul playlist in the background. I was comfortably positioned on my sofa, legs extended on the ottoman, staring into nothingness. I've always embraced this nomadic state. The company of solitude always led to conversations which stimulated my spirit and crowded my mind with thoughts.

Sometimes I wonder if I loved being with Miami more than anyone else. She was my feminine, the feminine spirit who complimented my masculine, creating the perfect balance which made me the man I am. Maybe this relationship with HER is what kept me unfaithful to anyone else. Do I fear commitment? How could I, as I am fully committed to HER. It's only with HER I can be completely me. I've learned so much about me solely because of HER. SHE doesn't judge me. I can cry with HER, dance out of rhythm with HER. When I talk to HER, SHE listens, and always gives sounds advice. SHE knows my heart. SHE'S always been there for me, SHE's my soulmate in this open relationshi... Solitude that is...

"Boom Boom Boom!!!!" the sound of someone banging on my door jarred me awake. I didn't realize I had fallen asleep. When I answered it there stood Miami! I definitely didn't expect to see her standing in my door way. She was clearly taking the news I dropped on her much differently than I expected.

That night was a blur. I couldn't believe she had flown to my house at the drop of a dime. We didn't argue. She was clearly pissed, but she kept it together, for the most part. I think she did break a few glasses in my kitchen, though.

We were already honest about everything, so there wasn't much explaining for me to do. She was upset because I had opened the door for conflict. Up until this point, there wasn't any with us. We hadn't argued about anything, really. Well, except for the one time I cooked her food in the same pan I had made chicken in without washing it. Apparently it was poison to a vegetarian. I thought it was completely ridiculous, but I yielded and let her have it.

Additionally, she still wasn't completely over her ex. Maybe I should say, she hadn't completely dealt with the trauma of the relationship. So the revelation about Karma's pregnancy was a trigger for her. She ended our relationship that night.

It’s important to keep in mind we had never discussed being in an exclusive relationship until this point. When she showed up on my doorstep, there was no questioning what she wanted. Why hadn't she communicated it to me? Maybe she was waiting on me to make the first move. I had thought about it... I just didn't know if our dynamic would change with us being long distance. It wasn't difficult when we didn't have expectations, but if we committed to being exclusive, would everything change? Would trust become an issue?

12

PHOENIX

October 19, 2018

At this point I really don't know what I'm going to do next. I think I just need some time alone. I'm trying to stay positive when thinking about Karma and the baby, but it literally feels like I'm in the twilight zone. How could everything go from going so good to chaos in the blink of an eye? Hell, I guess that's why it's called chaos. In reality, I know I have no one to blame but myself. I know I'm not an innocent victim here. I'm refusing to sit around and drown in guilt...

I just found out Karma lost the baby. I went to be with her and she told me, "I bet you're happy!" ... WTF! I get it, I didn't want a baby, but nah... I wouldn't wish trauma like that on anyone. Not like this... plus

I had already come to terms with actually having a baby with her. I didn't argue with her about it. It wasn't the time or place. In fact, there will never be a time and place for that conversation. I realize she doesn't really know me at all... Maybe she was just being emotional, but still...This time Karma was definitely being a bitch.

Love isn't all rainbows and sunshine
this ball of energy
the light it brings,
blinding,
temperamental,
rising and falling,
intense,
intent upon peeling back the
layers of me
I ain't ready to expose
making me sweat
or cry,
then leaving me dry
gasping for air
no shade,
but sometimes rainy days
are where the best
love is made.

A few weeks had passed and I was really in my head. If you would have seen me, you would have been none the wiser. I was a true artist at masking my feelings, but realistically, I was going through it.

I decided to reach out to Jean. We had always been good at talking to each other and I wanted a woman's perspective on things. She invited me over and I obliged. Bad idea. As soon as I got there I was like "Fuck!" She looked really good and she smelled good too. I kept my cool. I was good at it, acting like nothing was up. I just kept thinking "Please don't get hard." I should have just left, but I didn't. I really did want to talk to her.

"How are you?" she asked.

"I'm good." I wasn't ready to dive into what was on my mind. She took the lead and started talking about what was new in her life. Jean was a talker. I knew it and it didn't bother me. By the time she finished talking, I really didn't want to share what was on my mind anymore. Plus, I kept periodically thinking about wanting to have sex with her. I really didn't want to be that guy. I didn't go over there to have sex.

I was doing a good job at controlling myself. I showed no signs of even wanting her. But then she asked me, "Do you want to have sex? It's been a while for me and I haven't been ready to have sex with anyone else. I just want to cum and I'm tired of doing it myself. Plus we have always been good at it."

I didn't say anything at first, we had been here before. You know, attempting to have sex with no strings attached. It never really worked, mostly because we would keep having sex. She sounded different this time. She didn't sound desperate or like she couldn't have sex with someone else. She could if she wanted to. She literally had just finished telling me about a few dudes trying to get at her. Her words were very matter of fact.

I was a little thrown off, but was also not in a good head-space. The hard exterior I portrayed was now more literal than figurative. I won't say I gave in to her. That isn't fair. I think a part of me had an idea it could possibly happen. So... I agreed. Afterwards, there was no cuddling, no kissing, just a hug and a goodbye. Our once strong connection had been reduced to a moment of weakness.

I didn't necessarily feel bad about what happened. Admittedly, I enjoyed her physically. It felt different. There was a disconnect which hadn't been there in the past.

The next few days were kind of a blur. We talked a few more times, but our conversations had an air of dissonance. Mostly about the past, things which had transpired between us, or about some newfound realization in her life. I did more listening than talking. I never got around to telling her what I really wanted to talk to her about. It felt pointless. Jean and I could never go back to having a friendship like the one we had in the beginning. Too much had happened. Maybe in some distant future, but for now, the realization had finally set in.

~~Jean Grey~~ Phoenix,

I was going to call, but figured I'd just text it, that way you don't have to respond. Hell, you may not even read it now that I think about it. Anyways,

I was thinking about our last conversation, things I said, things you said. I initially called you because I was really feeling some kind of way, seeing you and everything, then I felt confused, etc...

As we talked and you started expressing yourself, I was

thrown back... in a good way... you sounded so different and confident, like you had clarity. I could do nothing but just agree with what you were saying.

After we got off the phone, I still felt incomplete. But you expressed how you felt about being friends and not needing closure, etc... So I didn't want to continue the conversation, really. It seemed just best to let it go. You are in a much better place and me inserting myself without the things you are looking for only creates problems, emotionally, mentally and induces stress...

I say all of this to say, I was meditating on you the last few days and today it just clicked...

The things I heard you say, your clarity, goals, intentions, your focus on positivity and your health, you recognizing AND claiming your self-worth, you realizing you're not alone, seeing your impact on the world around you, the confidence in which you spoke... I was like that, that right there, that's it...

It's funny how the Universe works, we've said it so many times. I didn't leave you because I thought I was doing you any favors. I'm not in ANY way trying to boost myself about this, it's the UNIVERSE.

Anyway, I didn't leave you because I thought I was doing you any favors. I legit left because I felt we weren't growing together. There was the aspect of realizing you had to let go and some other factors as well. Now, there's growth... not just in you, in myself as well, but I certainly recognize it in you.

I was really feeling down lately. I was not in a good mental space, but when I had this realization, it made my day, it was like the light bulb came on.

Everything happening is supposed to happen. If we would've just continued as we were, without the insight we have now, we still wouldn't have grown... but now, growth. I'm not saying it to say we ARE or AREN'T supposed to be together, I'm just saying, whatever the Universe has planned for us, this is a part of the journey. I really needed to come to the realization. I was definitely headed on a downhill slope and I was struggling to get refocused.

I just wanted to share with you. I will stop with the messages. I can stop wondering and worrying. The Universe is a true comedian, so I can only smile.

For as much as I loved you,
the moment I let go of you
I wanted to forget you.
But I knew you would always be there.
A piece of you embedded in me,
like a bullet next to my spine
unremovable
but I can move on.

13

CHASTITY

<u>October 20, 2018</u>

I've always heard people say men and women can't be friends. I think without self-respect and discipline it holds true. Sometimes I listen to Steve Harvey in the morning and he often goes on these rants about how it's impossible for a man and woman to be friends. His reasoning is a man will always jump at the opportunity to have sex with a woman.

There is partial truth to it, not even gonna lie. He does a lot of generalizing and reflecting on the weaknesses of his past experiences. He portrays them as the image of all men. It's such bullshit when he does it, or when anybody does it, to be honest.

The truth in the statement is based on our biological make-up and cultural conditioning. We are predisposed to be drawn to what attracts us. What I disagree with is the complete disregard for the ability of a man to grow spiritually.

He, like so many others, pours this negative energy into the world. He builds a narrative which actually perpetuates negative behaviors. The idea it is impossible for men to control themselves does more damage to the male psyche than good. If I'm led to believe I am predisposed to perpetuate toxic behavior, why would I even waste energy trying to change? It's basically like saying I'm an addict and the best thing I can do is learn to cope with my addiction. I can't genuinely reach a higher level of self. It feeds into the destructive connotations of masculinity and doesn't leave room for growth.

In my opinion, it's about being aware of myself and what level of maturity I'm at. I need to be intentional with my choices and the situations I put myself in. Being secure in who I am and having self-respect and respect of others is important. All these things lead to the ability to maintain positive platonic relationships with people I simultaneously find physically attractive. Most importantly though, is my spiritual growth.

I've learned not to allow my urges to control me and platonic relationships are able to occur.

Don't get me wrong, acting like this has not always been the case! Obviously, it's not something I learned overnight, nor is it like riding a bike. It isn't a "once you learn it, you got it" type of lesson. It's something I consciously and consistently work on. I'm always looking to be my best self.

Do I still have urges? Yes. At times they're stronger than others with certain people. But the more I practice self-control, the less those thoughts infiltrate my mind. While I can't control every thought, I do have full control over how I react to my thoughts.

Having a certain level of respect for myself makes me not want to let myself down. It becomes less about not wanting to hurt other people and more about me not wanting to dishonor myself. After working hard to be the person I want to be, I really don't want to throw all my work away. I really feel good about myself.

Additionally, when I truly respect someone else and I know they are not in a position to engage with me physically, I honestly prefer to protect their peace as well.

I met Chastity when I was in the Army. I was in D.C. on orders and she was stationed there. She had been assigned as one of the chaperons for our group. She was an amazon. Tall and curvaceous with almond eyes. She was a gorgeous woman. She had this sexiness about her that was captivating.

We flirted, a lot, a whole lot, more than what was excusable. I was still married at the time. We didn't cross the line, though. Not just because of her, either. But because of me. I didn't want to take it there. We had really good conversations and shared a lot of things with one another.

It wasn't a situation in which we talked every day or anything. It was when we did talk, we had in depth conversations.

Over the years we would meet up every now and again. There were a few times she made a pass at me and vice versa, but we always checked each other, respectfully. I think we both realized the sex wasn't worth the risk of our friendship. Sometimes I would even spend the night at her house if we hung out and it was too late for me to drive home. I met her daughter and a few of her friends. Perhaps, if the stars had aligned differently, we would have tried, but it just wasn't the case and we were both cool with it.

I have always appreciated Chastity and I'm sure the feeling is mutual. We can go months without talking, but it doesn't seem to change anything. We just pick up where we left off. She is truly a friend. She is who I should have called instead of Jean. I eventually did, and of course she helped put things in perspective. After letting me know what a dumb ass I was for sleeping with Jean again and expressing her empathy about Karma, she asked me a simple question:

"What do you want? If you want Miami, which it seems like you do, hell, you were talking about her months ago, then why you playing? You seem happy when you talk about her. I haven't heard you talk about other women like you do about her. You need to figure out what you want. Sounds like you playing to me." The thing about Chastity is, she always kept it a stack. Since there were no underlying intentions, I knew it was always real.

She had my head beating and my heart thinking.

"You're right," was all I could really say.

If I vibe wit you,
then I'm willing to ride wit you.
If I'm willing to ride wit you,
I'm willing to die wit you.
If I'm willing to die wit you,
then I'm willing to spread my wings and fly
wit you,
get high wit you,
face my fears - sky dive wit you,
show you my truth is not to lie wit you,
but to get "write" by you, and read minds wit you,
open my eyes, watch the world wit you,
maybe cry wit you,
watering me so I can grow like vines wit you,
bitter your sweet,
red wine wit you,
maybe dine wit you,
lighting these candles when it gets dark,
shine wit you.

14

PURSUING HER

A few days later I received a phone call from a friend of Trouble's, a.k.a Miami's. For some reason she felt it her place to "tell me about myself."

I didn't agree with a lot of things she was saying, but I respected it. I knew she was trying to protect her friend. What she didn't know was she did spark something in me.

In the mist of her talking, which eventually turned into Charlie Brown gibberish, I realized Miami's friend was fighting for her. So why wasn't I? Nah! I wasn't letting her off the hook easy. I mean yeah, the situation was sticky, but we were both playing the same game. I wasn't going to let her run off, just because we no longer had a perfect record. I was going to shoot my shot. Again.

The guilt and excuses which motivate you to apologize mean nothing until you realize personal growth and what to do next. They are the only things which justify your previous mistakes.

I thought maybe if I wrote to her, I could get her attention. Hell, I was always good with words. I would just pour out my truth and hope she would listen.

I was writing U to "write" my wrongs
O how I knew being with U should have
been OUI
yet I moved so individually
singled U out
kept U from becoming Us
yet tried to pluralize monogamy.
I was loving you the way love had conditioned
me
instead of loving you unconditionally
maybe subconsciously I believed
no one deserved the burden of falling in love
with me
because secretly I lusted polygamy
but she refused to marry me
when she saw the way I loved you
and recognized the change in me.

I don't want to sound cliche,
so I won't begin by saying I love you,
but through you I've learned how to love myself.
I'm not saying I need you to complete me,
but you tie my loose ends
you are who I am "knot,"
the complement of me,
compensating for what I
haven't paid enough attention to see.
I don't need you to be content with me

I'm asking you contend with me,
stand in my corner
see the fight in me.
I don't need you to compromise you
to commit to me,
but don't compromise our we.

I'm not going to tell you I love you.
I'm asking you to let me show you,
without allowing my ego to be my ruler.
I won't measure the love you deserve
proportionally to material things.
I don't want to be cliche
and simply tell you I love you.
I'm asking that you let me be love's Echo
through what I do.

I don't know if I can give you what you want,
but I can give my "reel,"
when the camera stops rolling.
I want you to see me when the curtain closes,
when the lights go out,
the mask comes off,
let you be drawn into the genuine me
by exhibiting the scars my naked truth possess
then you can decide if you want to risk
a prick from the thorns
of these wild roses.

I'm trying to be on some.
You are not cut like me,
and I am not cut like you,

but we belong together.
A perfect fit,
tessellation type shit,
beyond stars, we Super Novas,
constellation type shit.
On some, extra comfortable,
deep conversations over porcelain bowls,
cause you can't get me out your system,
constipation type shit.
On some, you're in your space and I'm in my space,
but the space between Mars and Venus is a gravitational bond,
stronger than any separation type shit.
On some, I'm the sun and you're the moon,
light up each other's world,
illumination type shit.
Tell me,
is you wit that shit?

Let's take the time spent to reinvest,
by taking the accumulation of our best assets,
the sweat equity put into our hearts and mindsets.

<u>November 2, 2018</u>
Nothing I try to write seems to be coming

out right, and honestly, I don't know if I can make this shit work. I feel like I have to try something, cause I'm not ready for this to end. I believe we can make this work. I ain't buying her no gift, though! I did that before and regretted it.

I remember when Sheba found out about Jean, I purchased her a ring as a token of starting fresh. The truth was, I was trying to do something to make her happy enough to forgive me, or to distract her from my transgressions.

I don't regret buying the ring financially, but every time I looked at the ring, I realized it didn't possess the value it should have. It reminded me of the one ring from Lord of the Rings: me bonding my manipulative powers with it to influence her and control the narrative of our relationship.

I don't want to repeat the past, so a gift is out of the question. But I can't just keep calling her like a fool either. She gonna start thinking I'm bat shit crazy! It will give her even more of a reason to distance herself from me. If I am going to get her attention, I have to do something drastic.

I BOOKED A FLIGHT TO MIAMI. I didn't tell her I was coming. I was just going to show up. Not at her doorstep though, on some creepy ass Love Jones vibe. I know people love the movie, but that shit was out of line. Who just shows up at someone's doorstep talking about, "I got your address off the check you wrote." WTF. LOL. NO WAY. That shit wasn't romantic. Instead, I got a hotel for the weekend down by the beach. When I got into town I called and left a message.

"Hey, I was just calling to let you know I'm here in Miami. I don't know if you are willing to come see me or not. I miss you. I want to talk to you. I'll be here for the weekend. I'm going to text you the address. Hopefully you show up, if not I understand."

I spent the day bar hopping and meeting some of the locals. Drowning my anxiousness in libations and meaningless conversations with people I had no intention of ever talking to again.

This one guy kept talking to me. The conversation started off about football. His vibe started to feel weird, though. I wondered if he was gay. It didn't matter to me, to be honest. As long as he didn't make a pass at me, or say some weird shit, I was cool. I figured I would start talking about Miami. I referred to her as "my girl." This would let him know I wasn't gay without me having to get the uncomfortable point across. Plus, I didn't really know if he was or wasn't. It hadn't been confirmed. Either way, when I referred to Miami as "my girl" I liked the way it sounded. It resonated with me. And then I saw her walk in, as if the Universe had been waiting for me to speak her into existence.

He asked me if she was my girl.
The audacity.
She's her own woman, actually

a Queen to me,
but she belongs to no man
as not even the King I am
has dominion over her presence.
She's God in body,
speak of her in reverence.
So yes, she walks with me
and talks with me.
We share the same space and energy,
but she's definitely not a possession to me,
nor is she a girl to me,
but she is with me because
I am the one with whom she has chosen to be.

My words walked through her mind.
My touch crawled up her spine.
My erection ran between her thighs.
I nested with her
love birds
singing love songs
with intertwined tongues
dancing to the rhythm of African drums
in sync
our beats
sounded as one.

I want to say she's mine
not possessively
like she belongs to me
but she's mine because
she's part of me inevitably
not physically
but mentally and spiritually

not like, mine solely, but soulfully
not by my choice
but because she was chosen for me
and we vibin' cosmically
on that Universal energy
her and me.

15

HER

<u>November 29, 2023</u>

I'm still learning about love, about myself, about HER. I've come to realize this course has no end, it's life long, all open notes, I just have to find the answers.

The irony of this class is it's a mandatory course, not an elective. Yet I won't receive any credits for taking it. There's no syllabus, no graduation date. I'll just keep taking it, semester after semester, each time learning something new, or not. I can either wake up dreading going to class, or learn to truly look forward to it. The latter has occurred for me. I have become fully engaged, recognizing it's significance in my life.

Suddenly learning has become fun. I now realize I am actually the creator of my own *course, my higher power, the facilitator. I would like to say, "if I knew then what I know now," but how would I have ever met HER? Everything I have learned so far has been to prepare me for this, for HER. I began to pour into HER and she poured into me.*

God said, "Let there be light," and there was light.
And so the evening and the morning were the first day.
And on the next day
God looked at the morning sun and saw it was good,
but realized the morning would be better with coffee.
Thirsty for perfection God
decided to grind together
beauty and intellect,
spread seeds on Ethiopian grounds
in-coincidentally
sowing the fabric of our existence
in this native soil nutrient rich with our roots
our family tree stems from
an Arabica
and she must be the berry
picked and kissed by the sun
dipped in hot water
the bittersweet sweat that dripped off God's brow,
Filtered through the clouds

a brewing storm
she's stunning
cupped lightning
sweetened with star dust
fuck a Starbucks
she tastes like heaven scent.
And God called her coffee
C-O-2 , ff's and ee's,
God's Breath of fresh air
//inhale//
smells like Kaffa Buna
aroma strong
hits like iron fists
brewed and roasted just right.
She fiery
soul savory
flavory, fiercely.
//snap//
Her spirit loves fiercely
gives off this energy
that makes mankind fein for her caffeine
her mind, java bean rich
within a hardshell
headstrong.

Every morning I yawn a silent scream for coffee
her warm opens my pores
energizing me
she pours into me intimately.
I love waking up and smelling the coffee.
I like my coffee bean black
lack the additives,
no sugar

no cream
organic
body so robusta,
melanin thick
skin cappuccino soft
the perk in her breast
Just right for my firm grip
So I reach and grab this cup of coffee.
I sip.
Her flow of melted mocha
//hot//
puckers my lips.
We french ground kiss,
intense, espresso shot strong,
so intoxicating.
I'm addicted,
a coffeeholic.
I get high off her Jamocha
//snap//
she a pick me up
she's vital to my vitality
warms me internally
enhancing my fertility
//OK//
I do like a splash of hazelnut
in my coffee,
but not a latte
still café noir.

I've heard men say,
"You shouldn't drink too
much coffee, try tea,"
and to that I say,

*“the Devil ‘sips tea’”
cause even he knows
God is a Barista.
What I mean is,
God set the Bar with a sista,
so without my God
there's no coffee
and without my coffee,
MY GOD,
what is life?*

*And on the next day
God created man,
from the dust,
and looked and saw
this creation was good,
and so we were gifted
and woken up
with a freshly Brewed cup of coffee.*

*We were both ten toes down.
What I mean is,
what we shared was "in-tens."
A "pair-a-dime" shifting our perspectives
into this unforeseen reality
where it all suddenly made "cents,"
that is, it changed everything.*

I'm not saying she's my sunrise,
it has dawned on me how
the light that she brings,
she changes my hue, my atmosphere,
I'm mesmerized by ribbons
in the sky,

I'm not saying she's my moonlight,
I feel drawn to her,
she drafts me in this gravitational pull,
raises waves of emotion,
that greet me with a high,
....

I'm simply saying that
she is the best part of my day,
I look forward to the eve,
that I want to spend nights with,
then wake up
to beautiful mornings

She asked me when I fell in love with her.
so I told her,
"I loved you in the moment between
when everything was stopped
and started revolving in a different direction
in time
in the blink of an eye
between inhale and exhale
in the moment of silence between heart beats
on the bridge where unconscious thought
entered my conscious mind
where nothing was supposed to exist
before the continuum of space-time
where nothing matters.
It was in the moment,
our energies found a way to collide,
stardust you and I,
I loved you from the very beginning.

2254.
It only took one time to see you with my 2 eyes,
but I swear I've fallen in love with you 2255 times.
Mathematically speaking,
love & reasoning doesn't seem to synchronize
it defies logic
but who's counting,
on anything
but opening my eyes

in sync with tomorrow's sunrise
so I can lay them upon you
at least one more time
2256...
2257...
2258 ...

She was my out of body experience
the prefix to my logical reasoning
lovesick with this emotional virus
the root of my irrational thought
or the coefficient beside it.
I was riding the wave, Poseidon,
my mind, body and soul, my trident
drowning her in my sex, energy, and intellect
keeping her deep in thought
her morning meditation,
so I could get to know her inside out
touch her soul to relieve any doubt
as she inhaled and exhaled me
we were both on this natural high
free from society's pesticides
so my third eye could finally see
the true hue of her Aurora
view her above the atmosphere.
She was my out of body experience,
so I could see myself loving her
from this new perspective of mine.

I don't need you to be the girl of my dreams.
I want you to meet me in this unscripted reality
and be the woman who inspires my dreams.

I don't want you to submit to me
just be willing to give me the best of you
in exchange for the best of me
so that the best of you strengthens the worst of me
and vice versa.
Forget submission, let's engage in an exchange of
power
to find a balanced position
scale down the weight of adversities
recalibrate where we stand so we can transition
and meet in the middle somewhere.

I don't need you.
I want you.
But my want for you,
is everything that I need.

I'm not just in to you.
I'm trying to be in tune with you
listening to you
then adjusting my notes in G-clef,
the right keys to open euphoria's door
and get high with you

crescendo with you
lie with you
falsetto with you
strike the right chord
harmonize with you
in the tempo of you.
I can be the King who
arranges an unforgettable melody
synchronizes with you
orchestrate a color of music with you
make a band named "Spectrum" with just the
right tones of you
I want to get in rhythm
and remix the blues with you.

She was both my heroine and my heroin,
my admiration and addiction,
either way she had me flying high.

Either I fell in love,
or into her gravitational pool
where I was held down, deep
into the depths of her,
my lungs
burned for a breath
until I learned to breathe her.

She just was
and so was I
so we just were
naturally being
and became
to be
We.

I am everything I need.
She is everything I want.
& We,
Well,
everything is everything.

16

LOVE

So, how do I define love?

First let me say, I don't think I can define love for YOU as some grand revelation. Understanding love is about the experience of life. I can only share my experience of love and you will determine against your own experience, what you believe love is and isn't.

How we ~~define~~ experience love is situational. A man can kill another man to protect his family and some would call it love. However, to the family of the deceased, it instigates hate. We can all claim to believe in the same God, but in war, both sides believe the same God loves them more than the other. Their actions are in the name of God.

So how can love truly have a definition? A single action can incite a feeling of love and hate at the same time.

This is where I believe we falter. We try to put love in a box only to witness it implode from the pressure we put on ourselves to try and understand it. It explodes from the complex arrangement of elements we think it requires.

We are saddened by the perplexity of it all, left to feel uncomfortable with our inability to maintain control, embarrassed by our exposed ignorance. We spend so much time trying to understand love, as opposed to just allowing ourselves to experience it. We can't explain love anymore than we can explain God, or existence itself. It just is.

Love to me is simple, it's energy. Energy which causes an involuntary sensory or emotional experience. We are all networked into this energy. The response we have to it is transferred to the people around us. They then experience the response as either positive or negative.

This explains why we think we are doing something out of love, but the person experiencing the energy may receive it as pain or hurt. The energy we give is based on how we have learned to respond to the experiences in life which are similar.

Defining love has to be based on our individual experience. This is why in writing this book, I simply wanted to share MY experience of love. Somewhere within these experiences, scattered throughout the pages of this book (depending on how you chose to decipher it,) lies a defining moment for you. For each of you it will be different, but either way, it's all love.

Love me as I am,
because the ugly truth is we are not the same
but the reality is
what makes US so beautiful.

Self love is the preparation necessary to give love
and giving love is what's required to receive love.

Love just appeared
unapologetically uninvited,
and let herself in.

Love and Logic,
two ends of a see-saw
a paradox
one without the other is unorthodox
destined to fall
they require balance
logic without love is chaotic
love without logic
psychotic
logic can't make sense of love
love has no sense of logic
yet the only logic that ever seems to make sense
is to just love.

Sometimes I just want to be lazy
and actively love you
by spending time with you
doing absolutely nothing
because sometimes
that nothing means everything.

I love you and me independently,
I mean like,

I don't let how much I love you
nor how much you love me
determine how much I love me
as I will always love me exponentially.

We must make love the adhesive substance
between us
otherwise how could we ever bond
unless we just love lying in the loose grip of lust
slipping through her sweaty palms
caused by that hot & sultry wet
we confuse with tea & honey.

I love fiercely but gently
infinitely but explicitly
courageously but cautiously
unconsciously but logically
silently but illustratively
freely but selfishly.

I found myself
when I learned to love myself
and I LOVED LEARNING!

Love is me finding
the trust to give you my heart
despite the fact

it was you who made me lose my mind.

Love is not a feeling
because if love is the feeling,
then what causes me to feel?

Love is not determined
by who you're with
it's determined by who you become.

Love is universal energy
both strength and weakness.

Love is not illogical,
it's the logic which makes your crazy make sense.

Love just is.

EPILOGUE

I call her Queen
because I identify the greatness in her
how she loves both herself
and her people equally.
I call her Queen
because of her ambition,
her love,
her creativity,
and conscious mentality.

I call her Queen
because she is what inspires me
emotionally and spiritually.
She is the definition of femininity,
the perfect combination of beauty,
intellect and sexy.
She would be a Queen to me,
even if she weren't with me,
as I see her independent
of who she is with me;

A Queen doesn't NEED a King
to justify her status as royalty.

I call her Queen
as a reminder of the King I need to be,
to continue to vibrate in her space,
transferring eminent energy.

~

When a King recognizes his Queen
and a Queen recognizes her King
it elevates their state of being.
He recognizes she doesn't idly stand behind him
she's positioning to push him.
She recognizes he's not egotistically standing
before her
he wants to be her warrior
escorting her.
She doesn't kneel beneath him
she's moving to uplift him
he is not above her
he's adjusting her crown.
He be head,
she be locks,
he be hope,
she be prayer,
he be rock,
she be gem,
fire and water,
earth and wind,
their bond combines
to bind

the perfect element.

~

I don't want to simply be enough for you.
I want you to want more from me
so we can continue to see
what this can grow to be.

~

Now what we came here to do is more than love
more than me simply telling you
I do.
It's a transformation from the fantasy
of how love is often defined
into this reality
of us intertwined
and molded into one
manipulated by the hands of trust
formulated by God's design.
This is an endless infatuation of desire
to simply be in your presence
for my soul to bask in the essence
of you
eager to quench
any inclination of your thirst
to love you the most
when you're at your worst
to be your rock
your pillow
the goose bumps running down your arms
when you think of me

you are the purpose
of my existence
my attraction before
I could see
you are the words
that define
me.

Supplied with just the right ingredients
to complete the recipe
baked in the heat of passion
watch us rise
and get high in the mist of our souls
open our third eye
so we can see the world
outside this human disguise.

I'm heavy with anticipation
of the beginning of a bond that's endless
generated by an appetite
for your sweetness
that has me addicted
so let this be my intervention
and I'll be rehabilitated
with a constant dose, of you.

Let's jump this broom
and never come down
let me love you more today
than yesterday
let's live this fairytale

on cloud nine
let the rhythm our heart beat
be measured in light years
transcending time
let this love never grow old
let's be two halves of one sphere
pouring into each other's bowls.

What we came here to do
is more than love
more than me simply telling you
I do.
This is me giving my all
to be one with you
so look into my eyes
and see the evolution of our souls
you'll see I'm letting myself go
to only have you to hold
to love
to cherish
to be the one whom I give my trust
til death do us part
as if that would be the end of us.

REVIEWS

Enjoyed this Book?

Reviews are incredibly powerful. Not only would I love to read your kind words, but I'd also appreciate your honest feedback.

As a self-published author, I don't have the same resources as large publishing companies, but I do have a supportive community of readers like you!

If you've enjoyed reading About Her please consider sharing it with your friends or taking five minutes to write a review on the book's Amazon page. Your support means the world to me.

Thank you,

Maurice L. Brown

ABOUT THE AUTHOR

Maurice L. Brown

Originally from Philly, Dr. Maurice "MoeFlowz" Brown is a Prince George, VA resident who has worked as an educator for over 15 years. A retired military veteran, a VSU alumni, a former VSU Mathematics Instructor, and current VCU Instructor at VCU's School of Business, Moe has ascertained a wealth of experiences and knowledge that he draws from in both his speaking engagements and his poetry. Moe is inspired by self-empowerment, self-love, growth, relationships, and community. His purpose is to deliver a message by exchanging energy with his audience and sharing relatable experiences. As a poet, he considers himself a mirror reflecting a portion of culture and society.

facebook.com/moeflowz

instagram.com/moeflowz

tiktok.com/@moeflowz02

www.ingramcontent.com/pod-product-compliance
Ingram Content Group UK Ltd.
Pitfield, Milton Keynes, MK11 3LW, UK
UKHW021936190726
13853UKWH00004B/1482

9 798991 233200